BASKETBALL ESSENTIALS

Ryan Goodson

HUMAN KINETICS

Library of Congress Cataloging-in-Publication Data

Names: Goodson, Ryan, 1986-

Title: Basketball essentials / Ryan Goodson.

Description: Champaign, IL : Human Kinetics, [2016]

Identifiers: LCCN 2016013088 (print) | LCCN 2016015253 (ebook) | ISBN 9781492519614 (print) | ISBN 9781492541301 (e-book)

Subjects: LCSH: Basketball. | Basketball--Training.

Classification: LCC GV885 .G66 2016 (print) | LCC GV885 (ebook) | DDC 796.323--dc23

LC record available at https://lccn.loc.gov/2016013088

ISBN: 978-1-4925-1961-4 (print)

Acquisitions Editor: Justin Klug; **Developmental Editor:** Anne Hall; **Managing Editor:** Nicole Moore; **Copyeditor:** Shannon Foreman; **Graphic Designer:** Julie L. Denzer; **Cover Designer:** Keith Blomberg; **Photograph (cover):** Human Kinetics; **Photographs (interior):** Neil Bernstein; **Visual Production Assistant:** Joyce Brumfield; **Photo Production Manager:** Jason Allen; **Art Manager:** Kelly Hendren; **Illustrations:** © Human Kinetics; **Printer:** Versa Press

Printed in the United States of America   10 9 8 7 6 5 4 3 2

The paper in this book is certified under a sustainable forestry program.

Human Kinetics

Website: www.HumanKinetics.com

United States: Human Kinetics
P.O. Box 5076
Champaign, IL 61825-5076
800-747-4457
e-mail: info@hkusa.com

Canada: Human Kinetics
475 Devonshire Road, Unit 100
Windsor, ON N8Y 2L5
800-465-7301 (in Canada only)
e-mail: info@hkcanada.com

Europe: Human Kinetics
107 Bradford Road
Stanningley
Leeds LS28 6AT, United Kingdom
+44 (0)113 255 5665
e-mail: hk@hkeurope.com

For information about Human Kinetics' coverage in other areas of the world, please visit our website: www.HumanKinetics.com

To all my loved ones: Mom and Dad
(thank you for always believing in me);
my beautiful wife, Ashley; my immediate family,
Chad, Caroline, Sadie, Billy, Debbie, Kerri, Alan,
Bear, and little Snicker; and my late grandfathers,
Bill Goodson and Byron Hass.

Contents

Acknowledgments

Special thanks to those coaches and mentors who have had an impact on me and have been leaders in my life. This book would not be possible without each of you. Thank you for inspiring me to work harder, be better, and believe in myself more. Thank you for teaching me the right way to play the game. Thank you for being a compass in my life. Your players are all truly blessed to have you as their coaches.

Ganon Baker

Brian Cantrell

Jason Capel

Bobby Cremins

Johnny Ely

John Lattimore

Matt McMahon

Richard Morgan

Buzz Peterson

Les Robinson

Ahmad Smith

Mark Thompson

I am most thankful for my relationship with my savior, Jesus Christ. He is my coach. I follow His playbook and talk to my coach through prayer. Basketball is of small importance in the grand scheme of things. One day the crowd will stop cheering. One day the ball will stop will bouncing. I am grateful to be on the team that will never lose. To God be the glory!

Introduction: Preparing to Practice and Learn

Welcome to *Basketball Essentials*! Thank you for investing in yourself and in this great game. Basketball is constantly evolving, and there is always something new to learn. The more I study the game, the more I realize what I do not know. The only way to excel is to constantly stretch, grow, reinvent, and improve; realize that you are a work in progress; and choose to be a lifetime learner. Whether you want to develop your knowledge of basketball fundamentals and improve your skills as a player or learn how to be a better coach and effectively teach, reach, and train the next generation of players, then you have come to the right place.

I have been blessed to train players all over the world from the youth level up to the NBA. I have worked with over 20,000 players since 2009, and conducted camps and coaching clinics in 30 states and 6 countries. With more than five million views on YouTube, I have produced numerous instructional DVDs and online training programs and have also worked around some of the best coaches and players in the game. I am thrilled to share all of my experiences with you.

BASIC OUTLINE OF THE BOOK

This book emphasizes learning by doing. *Form-repeat-compete* is a skill development principle and progression that I created specifically for this book to give players and coaches a formula for learning and mastering the fundamentals of basketball in a fun, efficient, and innovative way.

Form

First, you will learn the proper form and mechanics for each skill through a series of breakdown drills. To build a good foundation as a basketball player, you must have a good understanding of the fundamentals. The best way to learn and master these precious details is to practice the individual drills.

Repeat

Repeat these breakdown drills until muscle memory and correct habits are conditioned.

Compete

Once you have learned the form, you will begin a series of refinement drills. These drills are more comprehensive and gamelike, and most of them have a scoring component that allows you to measure your progress. This is where the real training begins! Steps 1 and 2 are about learning, and step 3 is about training, improving, and refining.

In addition to the aforementioned drills, each chapter has special sections to help coaches and parents become better teachers, leaders, and trainers (all of which are vital to the development of a good basketball player). *Basketball Essentials* has something for everyone.

FOR PARENTS AND COACHES

Whether you are a parent or a coach, the first thing you learn (usually out of frustration) is that teaching the game of basketball to youth players can be very challenging. I have personally faced every possible situation and obstacle that you can imagine, and I have worked with youth with limited attention spans, behavioral issues, and little athletic ability, coordination, or interest in the game. There are countless problems that you will face as a coach, but fortunately there are solutions to these problems if you approach your practices with energy, excitement, knowledge, and innovation. It's my job to properly equip you with different teaching methods and strategies that will assist in your instruction. I wish I knew these when I first began coaching!

TEACHING METHODS FOR YOUTH PLAYERS

When you introduce a new topic, follow this order of operations:

1. Articulate: explain the skill or drill using your words (auditory learning).
2. Demonstrate: actively display an example of the skill or drill (visual learning).
3. Participate: allow the players to participate and attempt the drill or skill (kinesthetic learning).

Progression

Even the most difficult basketball concepts and skills can be learned if you know how to teach in a progression. This book will outline numerous examples of progression. Players need to learn to play solo before they learn to play one-on-one. They need to master the layup before learning the jump shot. You will learn how to build and teach the fundamentals from the ground up.

Sound Cues and Acronyms

Sound cues and acronyms are an excellent ways to ensure that youth players retain the information you teach. With sound cues, you are packaging your teaching point in a rhyme, such as "if you dribble hard, the defense can't guard" or "if you stay low, your game will grow." With acronyms, combine the first letter of each teaching point to create a word. For example, when teaching shooting, many coaches use the acronym BEEF, which stands for

Balance

Eyes on target

Elbow in

Follow through

Sound cues and acronyms are fun ways to help players retain pertinent information.

Echo

One of the most important things to remember when working with youth players is that you must implement certain strategies throughout your practice to keep them engaged. Boredom is your enemy! One method I use is echoing; I always have players echo back all instructions. I also use echoing to keep players' attention. For example, I will say "Everyone give me two claps! Everyone give me two dribbles." Players must respond quickly and assertively to my command or there is a consequence.

Be a Choreographer

A great way to teach a complex skill or move is to train players like they are dancers, using numbers to break everything into easier-to-learn segments. For example, when teaching a common basketball finishing move called the Euro-pean step, provide the following instructions:

1. Stance
2. Forward step with right foot
3. Lateral step with left foot
4. Jump high and shoot

The player responds with the correct movements as you call out each number. Using numbers will help you to more easily identify mistakes and will expedite learning.

Let the Student Become the Teacher

Oftentimes when I am conducting a workout outside of the United States, I am faced with challenging ratios such as 30 players for every 1 coach. How can you properly teach in this setting and not become overwhelmed? Well, it's not easy, but it can be accomplished if you let your students become your teachers. Once I begin teaching a concept, I identify players who are doing the skill properly. I ask these players to be my assistant coaches and help those that are still learning. This is very beneficial for slower learners to whom I may not have the time to dedicate the necessary one-on-one attention. It's also beneficial for my assistant coaches because they have to step outside their comfort zones and instruct. I'm a big believer that you don't have a firm understanding of a concept until you can teach it.

Purpose

Remember, you are teaching skills and not drills. Drills are platforms for skills. It is important that every drill has a purpose and that players know and understand that purpose. Educating players about the purpose will help them perform more instinctively in games and will raise their basketball IQs.

Teach in Bullet Points and Not in Paragraphs

Less is always more; short and concise is the way to go. The more you talk, the less the players will remember. Try to construct your curriculum into quick and to-the-point messages.

Game-to-Instruction Ratio

To keep youth players engaged, it is important to keep a ratio of 5 minutes of activity for every 10 minutes of instruction. After every 10 minutes of instruction, I try to attach what we have just learned to a game that holds players accountable to the lesson.

Quiz

Education is the oxygen for success as a basketball player. At the end of each segment or practice, quiz your players on what they just learned. Reward correct answers with prizes.

The Big Picture

Teach the big picture first. When introducing a new topic, first demonstrate and allow players to participate in a gamelike drill. For example, when you introduce a motion offense to your players, quickly teach them a couple basic movements and then let them participate in a competitive five-on-five game. It will be chaotic, but if you don't show them the big picture, players will not understand how the skill applies to the game.

LEARNING TO LEAD

Back in 2009, I attended a coaching clinic in Orlando, Florida, with world-renowned skill-development coach Ganon Baker. I was a rookie coach, and I was hungry to learn from one of the best. At the time, Ganon traveled all over the world training players. He trained some of the NBA's best, and he had amazing passion and energy when he taught. This guy was on fire! His enthusiasm at practices was infectious. You could not help but be enthusiastic about the game, and life in general, when Ganon was in the gym. I remember vividly, on the last day of the clinic, Ganon called me over for a private chat. His tone was strong and assertive. He said, "Ryan, listen man. I've been watching you and you've got great potential. I believe that it's in God's will that you coach and teach this game. It's in your blood. It's in your DNA. You have to do it, and you can be every bit as good as me, or better. You understand?" After hearing these words from a mentor and someone I held in such high esteem, something changed in me. I wanted to work harder and be more committed. I wanted to challenge myself to be better, and, most important, I believed in myself more. That day, in that conversation, Ganon Baker was a leader. What if you could lead and inspire your players to be their best? What if you could help them apply this skill in their lives to be better players, students, sons or daughters, siblings, or friends? A true leader inspires others to work harder, be better (players and people), and believe more in themselves and the team.

I'm sure you can think of leaders in your life who have had an effect on you. As a coach, you have the awesome responsibility to lead. The following are some leadership rules I have learned through experience and observation.

Sell Rather Than Tell

I think sometimes there is a misconception that being a leader is like being a boss or a drill sergeant and that your job is to *tell* people what to do. This could not be further from the truth. Leadership is more about selling and less about telling. The best leaders inspire their players and package their instruction in such a way that it appears fun, rewarding, and attractive.

Motivate

A true challenge for any leader is to sustain their energy. Leadership is draining. You are constantly giving all that you have to get the most out of others. That is why it is so important to dedicate time each day to motivating yourself through reading a book, listening to music, or simply spending time with someone that gives you life. Remember, if you want to light someone else's candle and inspire them, *you* must be on fire.

Give High Fives

Lead your practice with high fives! You may not be the best or the most knowl-edgeable coach, but you can always lead your practice with positivity and encouragement. Believe it or not, there is a correlation between positive attitudes and winning! Something as simple as high five can make a difference in whether players believe in themselves.

Always Be Enthusiastic

Enthusiasm is contagious! If you're excited, your players will be excited. Enthusiasm is the genesis of greatness. Be enthusiastic!

Let Them Know You Care

This is a secret that I picked up from a McDonald's All-American player I trained. Being a McDonald's All-American is the highest honor that can be bestowed on a high school basketball player. He shared a rule with me that he implemented into his daily routine, and it helped lead his team to a national championship. He was the type of player that teammates loved to play with, and his teammates would do anything for him. How did he develop this kind of rapport? He made it a habit to have a 5- to 10-minute conversation with a different teammate each day. In that conversation, he made sure his teammate knew two things: He cared about them and he believed in them. Imagine how much that meant to his teammates and how this simple 5- to 10-minute conversation could impact your players! Apply this on the court and in your daily world if you want to make a difference in someone's life.

Be More Positive Than Negative

Keep a ratio of three positive comments for every one negative comment. Failure to do so can create a negative environment and lower morale.

Start and End Each Workout With a Message

Use motivational quotes or stories to apply basketball to life. A wise coach once told me that "[The message] is the most important part of the workout. It is the bigger purpose. It is why we coach."

Always Have Good Conduct

This should go without saying, but be sure to make good decisions on and off the court. Never do anything that you would not want printed on the front page of the newspaper. Be disciplined and understand that your decisions off the court can impact your players' willingness to follow you on the court. Lead by example and conduct yourself in a way that is worthy of being followed. You never know who is watching, and no one's life is so insignificant that others are not observing. Does your character lead others to their destiny or their destruction?

FIVE TRAINING TIPS FOR PLAYERS

I am not too far removed from being a player myself. I know how to teach the game, but I also remember what it is like to train. I easily relate to my pupils because I actually workout alongside them as I teach. Players, there are few things that I want to impress on you before we start learning and training in the following chapters. Understand that players all over the world are doing similar drills and working on similar concepts. The question is, how do you separate yourself from everyone else? The answer is simple, but it is not easy: You must train at a high intensity and have the patience and persistence to practice difficult skills *until you master them*; then you must maintain these habits and train over a long period of time to accomplish something significant. That being said, I have five short workout rules that I share with all the players I train, whether they are in the NBA or they are beginners.

1. Be the hardest worker on the court. The easiest way to change your game is to change your work ethic. Train at a high intensity and always train at game speed or faster.

2. Be the most enthusiastic player on the court. Your body is allowed to get tired, but your spirit never can. Lead your team in high fives, chest bumps, and encouraging words. There is always a spot on a team for someone with enthusiasm and positive energy.

3. Never give up! Do not quit! There is no limit to what you can accomplish if you continue to persevere. Failure and adversity are a part of learning.

4. Have higher standards for yourself than the world around you does. If you want more, you have to expect more. Set the bar high and pursue excellence.

5. Patience: Be willing to wait! There is no easy path to greatness and success. Boring, monotonous repetition over a long period of time is the key. Slow is fast! Appreciate and celebrate even the smallest improvement along the way, and be willing to wait for major progress.

Now that you are prepared to practice and learn and you have a basic understanding of how to teach, lead, and train, let's take an in-depth look at the fundamentals of the game.

Key to Diagrams

→ Cut or player movement

⊥ Screen

⇢ Pass

〜〜➤ Dribble

◁ Cone

Ⓒ Coach

① ② ③ Offensive player positions

Ⓧ1 Ⓧ2 Ⓧ3 Defensive player positions

Chapter 1

Dribbling

Dribbling is a no-excuses skill. You don't need a gym, a teammate, or a hoop to improve your ball handling; you simply need a basketball, a hard surface, and a strong work ethic. My experience has shown me that there are a lot of players around the world who excel at dribbling the basketball, but very few of them are proficient at driving. Being a great dribbler is a requirement for being a great driver, but not all great dribblers are great drivers. In this chapter on dribbling, I focus on building skills that will help you drive the ball and beat the defense. Dribble-drive skills put you and your team in an advantageous position. Players who can advance the ball past the defense create better shots for themselves, improve the percentage of shots for their teammates, draw more fouls, and collect more offensive rebounds. These are the motivations for being a great ball handler. I have observed coaches who spend hours teaching players the proper mechanics they need in order to become proficient shooters, but then they fail to teach the fundamentals and techniques players need to master dribbling and, as a result, driving. In the first section, I present the fundamentals of drills for understanding and retention. In the second section, I help you refine your skills for game success and mastery. Grab your basketball and follow along with me as you build your handles!

USE YOUR DRIBBLE, BUT DON'T LET YOUR DRIBBLE USE YOU

Useful dribbling beats the defense, alleviates pressure, and creates opportunities, but overuse or overdribbling generates more turnovers and results in lower field-goal percentages as well as apathetic and frustrated teammates. Use your dribble, but don't let it use you. Use it, but don't abuse it. How? Learn to use the dribble with a purpose. There are only four reasons to dribble the basketball in the game.

1. To Score

If you have an opening to the basket, see an unoccupied area, or have the advantage, use your dribble to separate from the defense and score.

2. To Create a Better Passing Angle or to Shorten a Pass

If your teammates are too far away and you don't feel comfortable throwing a long pass, or if you need a better angle to deliver your pass, use the dribble to assist you in completing that pass.

3. To Alleviate Pressure and Get Out of Trouble

If a trap comes or if the defensive pressure is too great, use your dribble to create space and to get out of trouble.

4. To Advance the Basketball up the Floor

If a teammate is not open for a pass, use your dribble to advance the basketball up the floor.

SAVE IT AND MAINTAIN IT

If you attend a youth basketball game, you are in for a wild and exciting scene. These players, who are still learning the game, compete as if it's game seven of the NBA Finals. Inevitably, you will see the following scene play out numerous times: Johnny receives a pass and immediately begins to dribble without any thought about why; then, to make matters worse, Johnny picks up his dribble before he has a solution, putting himself in a very desperate position that leads to a turnover. Once you begin dribbling, save that dribble and maintain it until you have a solution. Solutions include scoring or passing opportunities. Picking up your dribble without a solution will put you at an extreme disadvantage, so once you use it, don't lose it!

BE AMBIDEXTROUS

Ambidexterity is the ability to use either hand equally well. This is a non-negotiable fundamental. If you want to be a proficient ball handler, you must be able to dribble with either hand. You negate 50 percent of your options if you can dribble with only one hand. To shield the basketball from the defense with your body, use your right hand when dribbling to the right and your left hand when dribbling to the left. When performing the drills in this chapter, train with each hand. You must do this if you want to build true game handles. It has also been my observation that if you train with your weak hand, it will make your dominant hand better. So, if you are only willing to train with one hand, make sure it's your weak hand. The goal of training, however, is to not have a weak hand.

COIL UP

Basketball is played low; this is universal in the game. The only time you come out of your stance is when shooting, rebounding, attempting to block a shot, or simply sprinting up the court, and even those skills begin in a low stance. Whether on offense or defense, you're almost always in a stance with your knees bent, back straight, hips dropped, and feet shoulder-width apart. I call it being coiled up. Think about it: A rattlesnake is a deadly predator, but if that rattlesnake is not coiled up, then it's not as much of a threat. You won't be a threat to the defense as a ball handler if you're not coiled up, low, and ready to strike with a drive, shot, or penetrating pass. You will be faster and stronger and will have better balance if you are coiled up. How low should you be? Look at the numbers on the front of your opponent's jersey; your numbers should be lower than theirs. The lower player in basketball usually wins. Gain the advantage and become deadly to the defense by being coiled up.

RATTLESNAKE DRILL

Breakdown

Setup

- Use one player, one basketball, and one tennis ball.

Execution

1. The player pounds the basketball with one hand while repeatedly placing a tennis ball on the ground and picking it up with the nondribbling hand.

2. When placing and picking up the tennis ball, the player must bend at the knees and not at the back and maintain an athletic and low stance.

3. The player performs the drill for 30 seconds with each hand.

Coaching Point

The player should remain in a low and athletic stance for the duration of the 30 seconds, attempting to keep the eyes up and using peripheral vision to locate and retrieve the tennis ball.

FINGER PAD CONTROL: ABSORB THE BASKETBALL

To have total control of the basketball, make sure that no part of the palm comes in contact with the ball. Keep the basketball on your finger pads and fingertips, and spread your fingers as wide as possible to maximize your ability to control the

FINGER PAD DRILL

Breakdown

"...you should have enough space between the basketball ...y fit two fingers. When the basketball contacts only the ...assumes the position of a suction cup and is easily able to ...late the ball.

Setup

- Use one player and one basketball.
- The player is kneeling on one knee.

Execution

1. The player begins dribbling the basketball 1 to 2 inches (2.5-5 cm) off of the floor.

2. The player concentrates on keeping the palm off the basketball and manipulating the basketball using only the finger pads and fingertips.

3. The player performs the drill with each hand for one minute.

Coaching Point

If the player is having trouble keeping the palm off the basketball, stop the drill momentarily and have the player hold the basketball in their faceup palm. The player should then correct the hand position by allocating enough space to insert two fingers between the ball and the palm. Once this is achieved, the player can continue the drill.

EXTEND YOUR DRIBBLE

I tell players to dribble so hard that they put dents in the floor! NBA All-Star Chris Paul once said he dribbles so hard that if he let the basketball drift into the air, it would touch the ceiling. The best ball handlers in the game today all have something in common: they use the entire arm to create a quicker handle, not just the wrist. To use only your wrist to dribble is average, and you don't want to be average, you want to be exceptional.

The best ball handlers extend their elbows the same way players do when taking a shot or making a pass. This is called the *comprehensive release*. You should shoot, pass, and dribble with full elbow extension. Try it. Without a basketball, pretend that you are taking a shot and freeze your release at the top. Your elbow should be locked and extended. Now, make an imaginary pass and freeze your release. Your elbow should be locked and extended. To build an effective dribble, practice the comprehensive release and lock out your elbows on the dribble. Picture yourself as a boxer, using your dribble to damage the defense. A boxer's trainer will tell them to follow through with punches and to not just punch the target but to punch *through* the target. Knock out the defense by explosively pounding the dribble with full elbow extension. Some reasons you should practice the dribble release include the following:

- Ball quickness will make you a quicker player.
- You will have better ball control because the basketball is in your hand longer than it is out of it.
- A quicker dribble will help you more quickly read and react to the defense.

POUND TO THE GROUND DRILL

Breakdown

Setup

- Use one player and one basketball.
- The player has the basketball and is in a low and athletic stance.

Execution

1. The player makes 10 explosive pound dribbles with full elbow extension (figure 1.1a).
2. On the 10th dribble, the player pounds the dribble dead to the ground and locks out the arm in full extension to reinforce the dribble release technique (figure 1.1b).

Figure 1.1 Pound to the ground drill.

(continued)

Pound to the Ground Drill *(continued)*

3. The player then picks up the basketball and repeats steps 1 and 2.
4. The player performs the drill for one minute with each hand.

Coaching Point

To generate even more power on the dribble, the player should exhale assertively with each dribble. Studies show that exhaling increases strength, speed, and explosiveness.

USE YOUR SHIELD

Ball protection is of utmost importance for a ball handler. Your first responsibility is to maintain possession of the basketball. Be in the habit of shielding the basketball from the defense by using your nondribbling hand as a barrier between the basketball and the defender (see figure 1.2). When the defensive pressure becomes too great, it may also be applicable to shield the basketball from the defender with your entire body.

Figure 1.2   Proper use of the shield by the ball handler.

HIGH-FIVE DRILL

Breakdown

Setup

- Use two players and two basketballs.
- Each player has a basketball; players face each other with no more than an arm's length of space between them.

Execution

1. Each player begins with a stationary dribble in the right hand.
2. Players 1 and 2 exchange high fives with their nondribbling hands.
3. Players perform the drill for one minute with each hand.

Coaching Point

This is a fun drill, usually a player favorite, that will help reinforce the use of the nondribbling hand to shield the basketball from the defense.

PRACTICE COURT VISION

It doesn't matter how great a ball handler you are if you can't see the opportunities available to you on the court, such as an open teammate, a driving lane to the basket, and so forth. Players must play with great court vision and have an awareness of not only the defender, but also of the next level of the defense. It's not enough to just have your eyes up; you must use your vision efficiently. I teach players to maintain eye contact with the center of the court or the rim so they can see the entire court with their peripheral vision.

Setup

- Use one player and one basketball.
- The player dribbles the basketball near the top of the key while the coach (or a teammate) stands under the rim.

Execution

1. The coach or teammate gives the player a visual command by pointing right, left, forward, or backward; the player must then respond to the command (figure 1.3).

2. If the player is directed to move right or left, they step-slide with the dribble in that direction.

3. If the player is directed to move forward, they speed dribble forward.

4. If the player is directed backward, they backpedal with the dribble.

5. The player performs the drill for 30 seconds.

Coaching Point

It's not enough that players play with their eyes up; they must also keep their eyes fixed on the middle of the court so they can see the entire court with their peripheral vision. This drill keeps the visual focus on the middle of the court.

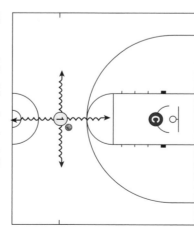

Figure 1.3   Idan Ravin drill.

BASIC DRIBBLING MANEUVERS

All ball handlers need to be able to create space from the defense. The five basic dribble moves discussed in this section will help you alleviate pressure from the defense and be poised and confident to make good decisions with the basketball. The fundamental ways to create space are as follows:

- Change your direction.
- Change your speed.
- Use the retreat dribble.

The checklists that accompany the five dribble maneuvers will help you understand each one.

Hesitation

The hesitation dribble is most commonly used when you are quickly advancing the basketball up the floor in transition and your defender is stationary or backpedaling. Review the following checklist for the correct order of operations when executing the hesitation dribble.

Hesitation Dribble Checklist

1. Speed dribble at the defense.
2. Come to a sudden stutter-brake stop.
3. Remain in your stance.
4. Keep your dribble to the outside of your body, not in front.
5. Shield the basketball with your nondribbling hand.
6. Take your eyes to the rim.
7. Pause.
8. Explode past the defense with a hesitation dribble (see figure 1.4).

Figure 1.4 Hesitation dribble. Notice that the player's feet are chopping.

Retreat

The retreat dribble is most commonly used to create space against an overly aggressive defender who is putting tremendous pressure on the ball handler. Review the following checklist for the correct order of operations when executing the retreat dribble.

Retreat Dribble Checklist

1. Enter a defensive dribble stance with your body between the defender and the basketball.

2. Point your inside shoulder to the defender's chest.

3. Keep your chin on your inside shoulder to maintain your view of the court.

4. Pound your dribble low and tight behind your back foot (see figure 1.5).

5. Take two retreat slide dribbles back.

6. Square your body to the defense and survey your options.

Figure 1.5　Retreat dribble.

Crossover

The crossover dribble is most commonly used when you are advancing the basketball up the court and the defender cuts off your angle. The crossover can be a vulnerable dribble because changing hands in front of the body directly exposes the basketball to the defense. It's important to only use the crossover when there is at least an arm's length of space between you and the nearest defender. Review the following checklist for the correct order of operations when executing a crossover dribble.

Crossover Dribble Checklist

1. Keep the dribble low and tight on the outside of your knee (figure 1.6a).

2. Cross the basketball low and below the knees to the opposite hand (figure 1.6b).

3. Cross the basketball long from outside one knee to the other.

4. Use your nondribbling hand to shield the basketball (see figure 1.6c).

5. Put your weight on your inside foot and explode past the defense.

Figure 1.6   Crossover dribble.

Between the Legs

The between-the-legs dribble is another move that is commonly used in advancing the basketball up the court and the defender cuts off your angle. Unlike the crossover, the between-the-legs dribble can be used even when the defender is close because the body serves as a shield as the basketball changes hands between the legs. Review the following checklist for the correct order of operations when executing the between-the-legs dribble.

Between-the-Legs Dribble Checklist

1. Keep the dribble low and tight on the outside of your knee (figure 1.7*a*).

2. Stop, sit, and split your feet.

3. Cross the basketball low and tight between your legs (figure 1.7*b*).

4. Use your nondribbling hand to shield the basketball.

5. Put your weight on your inside foot and explode past the defense.

Figure 1.7 Between-the-legs dribble.

Behind the Back

The behind-the-back dribble is another move that is commonly used in advancing the basketball up the court and the defender cuts off your angle. The behind-the-back dribble can be used when the defender is close because the body serves as a barrier as the basketball changes hands behind the back. Review the following checklist for the correct order of operations when executing a behind-the-back dribble.

Behind-the-Back Dribble Checklist

1. Keep the dribble low and tight on the outside of your knee (figure 1.8*a*).
2. Cross the basketball low and tight behind the back to the opposite hand (figure 1.8*b*).
3. Use your nondribbling hand to shield the basketball.
4. Put your weight on your inside foot and explode past the defense.

Figure 1.8   Behind-the-back dribble.

REACTION DRILL

Breakdown

Setup

- Use one player, one basketball, and two cones.
- The player starts at half-court with one basketball.
- The coach begins at the top of the key in the middle of two cones, as shown in the diagram.

Execution

1. The player attacks the outside of either cone with a speed dribble (figure 1.9).

2. At the line of the cone, if the coach does not move and cut off the player, the player continues in the same direction for a layup or a jump shot.

3. If the coach does slide and cut off the player at the line of the cone, the player makes a quick read and reaction and changes direction, attacking the middle of the cones for a jump shot or a layup.

4. The player repeats the drill using the crossover, between-the-legs, and behind-the-back dribbles.

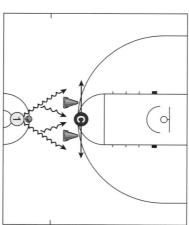

Figure 1.9 Reaction drill.

Coaching Point

This is a terrific drill to reinforce correct reads and reactions as a ball handler. In the game there is not always enough time to think; players must build instinctual habits in practice that enable them to react.

OPENING THE DEFENDER'S GATE

The two types of keys used to open a defender's gate are action keys and reaction keys. As a player, you must embody both of these dynamics.

Action Keys

Michael Jordan once said, "The defender is my puppet and they will do what I want them to do." In the action mode, the ball handler attempts to attack the defender with an offensive move in order to gain the advantage. For example, engaging the defender (left or right) with an offensive move to slide the defender's gate open creates an opening to the basket. You must have offensive moves that you can use against the defense. These moves can be used to elicit a particular reaction from the defense, thereby giving you complete control.

Reaction Keys

The speed of your dribble is important, but how quickly you can read and react to what the defense does is equally important. If they reach, quickly take advantage of their aggressiveness and counter with the correct reaction. For example, if the defender's hands are down, then it's man down; react by taking your shot. Oftentimes the best move is not a move, but rather a correct reaction.

REFLECTION DRIBBLING DRILL

Breakdown

Setup

- Use two basketballs and two players.
- Each player has a basketball; players face each other.

Execution

1. Player 2 must follow and mimic whatever type of stationary dribbling maneuver player 1 executes.
2. Players perform the drill for one minute; then they switch roles.

Coaching Point

This is a great drill to develop reading and reaction skills and to hold players accountable for dribbling with their eyes up. Pair your players by similar skill level to maximize the repetitions in the drill.

The First Step

After inserting your action or reaction keys into the defender's gate, you must learn how to gain the advantage on the defense and open the gate. No matter what type of offensive maneuver you use, you must beat the defender's feet with your lead foot, your shoulders, and the basketball on the first step by the defender. This requires taking a long and low step by the defender on your first step to the rim. If you beat the defender with these three things on the first step, you will gain the advantage and open the gate to the basket.

FIRST-STEP CONE DRILL

Breakdown

Setup

- Use one player, one basketball, and one cone.
- The player starts with a basketball in hand, and the cone is on the lane line.

Execution

1. The player executes 10 pound dribbles with one hand.

2. On the 10th dribble, the player drops low and takes a long step by the cone.

3. The player ensures that the lead foot, the shoulders, and the basketball are by the cone.

4. Once in this position, the player picks up the cone with the nondribbling hand (by bending at the knees, not with the back) and explodes with their dribble to the opposite side of the lane (figure 1.10).

Figure 1.10 First-step cone drill.

5. Once on the opposite side of the lane, the player repeats the drill and returns.

6. The player performs the drill for 60 seconds with each hand.

Coaching Point

This drill is important for all levels of play, but it is especially important for young female players who have a tendency to lead with the basketball and not with their feet. Proper mechanics and the order of operations in this drill will help any player to improve their driving skills.

CLOSING THE DEFENDER'S GATE: SEPARATION OR POSITION

Closing the defender's gate is a phrase that is commonly used when instructing players on escaping from their defender after executing an offensive move. The perfect conclusion to any offensive move is that the offense is able to gain and also maintain inside position between their opponent and the basket. Maintaining the inside position, or closing the gate, can be achieved by implementing the separation or position and pursuit of the rim techniques.

Separation

Once you've beaten the defense with a great first step, close the gate by using the basketball to separate. Your feet give you the freedom, and the ball helps you gain space from the defense. Push the basketball out to an unoccupied area of the floor that is in the direction you are headed. You can tell how explosive a player is by how much space they can cover with each dribble. Great drivers capitalize on the advantage they've created by opening the defender's gate and quickly separating from the defense. This puts stress on the next wave of defenders and produces scoring opportunities for the ball handler and their teammates.

Position and Pursuit of the Rim

This technique is often called the two Ps. It's a great technique that ends the foot race to the rim in only two steps, but it is not about speed. The first step is made by the defense and in a direction toward the rim, and the second step is directed behind the defense. For example, the ball handler should take a long right foot step toward the rim and by the defender's feet (figure 1.11*a*), followed immediately by a left foot lateral step to secure inside position between their defender and the rim (figure 1.11*b*). This technique puts the defender on the ball handler's back, giving them the inside position, and closes the gate. When this technique is applied, the game slows down, and this allows the ball handler more time to make correct reads and reactions to help defenders.

Figure 1.11 Close-the-gate technique.

FOUR QUARTERS DRILL

Breakdown

Setup

• Use one player and four cones, as shown in the diagram.

Execution

1. The player must complete all four quarters of the court as quickly as they can.

2. The player completes a layup in one dribble from the three-point line followed by completing a layup in two dribbles from half-court and then a layup in three dribbles from three-quarters court, and lastly a layup in four dribbles from the opposite baseline (figure 1.12).

3. Time the player from the beginning of the drill until the final layup is made. Record their time.

4. The player executes the drill with each hand.

Coaching Point

For an additional challenge, have the player attempt the drill with two basketballs by executing the appropriate number of dribbles from each spot with two basketballs. When arriving at the rim, the player should finish the layup with the basketball in the outside hand and simply hold onto the remaining ball.

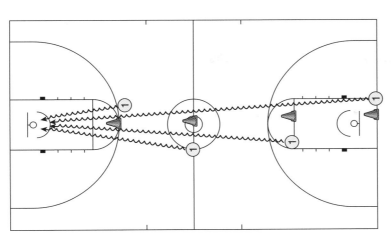

Figure 1.12 Four quarters drill.

CLOSE-THE-GATE DRILL

Breakdown

Setup

- Use two players and one basketball.
- Players line up side by side, shoulder to shoulder, with their toes pointed to the baseline. Player 2 (the defender) assumes the inside position between player 1 and the basket. Player 1 has the basketball and controls when the one-on-one game begins.

Execution

1. When player 1 moves, player 2 can move.

2. Player 1 is instructed not to separate and score but to first seek inside position and then pursue the rim by stepping across the body of player 2 with the inside leg (figure 1.13).

3. Players receive 1 point for every made basket and change possession of the basketball with each repetition.

Coaching Point

For simplicity, I tell my players that this movement is the same as boxing out; this gets them in the mind-set of fighting for inside position and not just dribbling the ball to the rim.

Figure 1.13 Close-the-gate drill.

PUTTING ON THE BRAKES WITH BALANCE

Players must be able to make sudden stops and remain on balance. I once observed a professional player working on his footwork, and he would stop so suddenly and precisely that I could smell burnt rubber from the soles of his shoes. The ability to stop is an undervalued skill; it limits turnovers and helps you play with more control and balance for the next play. There are three types of stops that I work on with players.

1. Brake Stop

A one brake stop is also referred to as a jump stop. To perform this stop, decelerate by jumping slightly into the air and then returning to the ground with two feet at the same time and coming to a balanced stop.

2. Two-Brake Stop

To perform this stop, decelerate by braking with two feet and come to either a sudden left foot-right foot stop or right foot-left foot stop.

3. Stutter-Brake Stop

To perform this stop, decelerate by chopping your feet to slow yourself from full speed and come to a balanced stop while maintaining the dribble.

RED LIGHT-GREEN LIGHT DRILL

Breakdown

Setup

- Use one player and one basketball.
- The player starts on the baseline with a basketball and waits for a command.

Execution

1. When the coach says "green light," the player accelerates at full speed up the court with a speed dribble.
2. If the coach says "red light," the player comes to a quick and on-balance stop.
3. The player repeats the drill for 60 seconds.
4. The player works on the brake stop, the two-brake stop, and the stutter-brake stop for 60 seconds each.

Coaching Point

The ability to stop and be on balance is an important skill. Make sure that when players come to a stop they are not leaning in any particular direction and their weight is centered evenly over both feet.

FLOOR GENERAL: COMMUNICATION

Imagine for a moment that you're the point guard on your team. You're in charge of advancing the ball up the court and starting your team's offense by completing a pass to a teammate on the wing. There is one problem: your teammates aren't open despite your ability to handle the basketball. How do you get the ball to the wing? Use a hidden and overlooked skill: your voice. A great floor general will give their teammates directives such as *ball screen*, *cut through*, and *dribble handoff*. Find your voice!

Fundamentals for Successful Basketball Communication

1. Call out your teammate's name.
2. Talk early and often, and use reminders.
3. Be specific with your information.
4. Speak in bullet points and not in headlines.
5. Speak loudly and with conviction, and have a confident tone.
6. Maintain eye contact.

COMMUNICATION DRILL

Breakdown

Setup

- Use six players and six basketballs.
- The players line up shoulder to shoulder. Each player has a basketball and begins dribbling.

Execution

1. On the coach's command, each player must switch basketballs with another player (figure 1.14).

2. Each time the coach says "switch," the players must switch with a different player.

3. If at any point one ball stops bouncing, the drill ends and there is a consequence.

Coaching Point

This drill reinforces an important fundamental that there should be no mistakes due to poor communication.

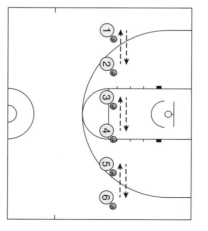

Figure 1.14 Communication drill.

MASTERING THE SLOW TO GO

When I was dating my wife, she lived in Harlem, New York. One time when I visited, she surprised me by taking me to the famous Rucker Park for a basketball game. The players played with such flair, creativity, and rhythm—a rhythm that many coaches would believe is a natural talent and can't be taught. But in my observations, I began to see a very basic commonality in the players' movements and timing. What made these players so hard to guard? They had mastered what I call the *slow to go*. They used exaggerated changes of speed, specifically in dribbling and accelerating around the court, to put the defense off balance. They would move unexpectedly between very fast and very slow, and then when the defense least expected it, they would *go* and explode by attacking the defense with a shot, drive, or pass.

SLOW TO GO DRILL

Breakdown

Setup

- Use one basketball and one player.
- The player is on the sideline with the basketball and in an athletic stance.

Execution

1. The player executes five high-intensity, low-pound dribbles and then five very slow, high dribbles.

2. Next, the player explodes with a speed dribble to the opposite sideline.

3. The player repeats the drill from sideline to sideline for one minute and then does it again with the other hand.

Coaching Point

Players must not be robots in this drill; they should try to have a different rhythm for each set in the drill.

REFINEMENT DRILLS

You now have a basic understanding of the fundamentals of dribbling and driving, so let's advance to refinement drills. Refinement drills are gamelike, challenging, and competitive. This is where the real training begins!

BASKETBALL SLAMS DRILL

Refinement

Setup

- Use one player and two basketballs.
- The player begins in a low and athletic stance and remains stationary.

Execution

1. The player begins by dribbling two basketballs at knee level as hard as they can, extending the elbows with each dribble.

2. On the 10th dribble, the player releases one of the basketballs into the air (with the goal of it hitting the ceiling) while maintaining a quick, low dribble with the other ball.

3. To score the drill, count how many times the player can pound basketball 2 at knee level before basketball 1 returns to the ground.

4. The player performs the drill for 30 seconds.

5. The player repeats the drill with the opposite hand.

Coaching Point

To work on court vision, the player's eyes should focus on the basketball in the air, not on the basketball in the hand.

Scorecard

Junior varsity: 1 to 3 dribbles

Varsity: 4 to 6 dribbles

All-conference: 7 to 9 dribbles

All-American: 10 or more dribbles

BOB HURLEY DRILL

Refinement

This drill is used to practice gamelike reading and reaction skills.

Setup

- Use two players, two basketballs, and one cone.
- Players stand on opposite sidelines; each player has a ball and begins to dribble with the right hand.

Execution

1. Player 1 and player 2 dribble toward the cone and each other at full speed.

2. When they arrive at the cone, player 1 chooses which change-of-direction move to execute: crossover, between the legs, or behind the back.

3. Player 1 performs the move, and player 2 must successfully mimic it (figure 1.15).

4. After completing the change-of-direction move, each player speed dribbles to the opposite sideline; then they repeat the drill.

5. Player 2 receives 1 point each time they successfully complete the move without breaking speed or slowing down.

6. Each player performs the drill for one minute and records their score.

Figure 1.15 Bob Hurley drill.

Coaching Point

This drill is meant to be completed at full speed. Players should not break speed or slow down, and faking is not allowed. The leader in the drill makes one decisive move and then exits. To elevate the drill, instruct players to make two or three moves before exiting.

CHAIR DRILL

Refinement

Setup

- Use one player, one chair, and one basketball.
- The player starts at the top of the key with the ball and the chair.

Execution

1. The player executes 10 pound dribbles with the outside hand.
2. On the 10th dribble, the player takes a long, low first step with the outside leg by the chair while hitting the chair with the inside hand.
3. The player then explodes to the basket in one dribble.
4. The player is awarded 1 point for every layup made.
5. The player performs the drill for one minute and records the score.
6. The player then repeats the drill with the opposite hand.

Coaching Point

Make sure that the basketball and the player's shoulders and lead foot are by the chair before the player separates to the basket for the layup.

Scorecard

Junior varsity: 1 to 2 layups

Varsity: 3 to 4 layups

All-conference: 5 to 6 layups

All-American: 7 or more layups

CHANGING SPEED DRILL

Refinement

Setup

- Use one player, one basketball, and four cones.
- The player starts on the baseline with the ball.

Execution

1. While dribbling, the player explodes to the first cone.

2. When the player arrives at the first cone, they stop and tap the cone with the nondribbling hand and then pause.

3. The player then explodes and repeats this move at each of the subsequent cones (figure 1.16). Make sure there is an exaggerated change of speed from fast to slow at each cone.

4. When the player arrives at half-court, they must turn around and repeat the drill with the opposite hand.

5. The player performs the drill for one minute.

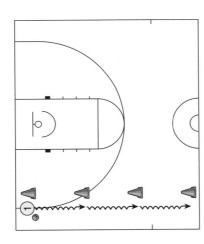

Figure 1.16 Changing speed drill.

Coaching Point

Oftentimes when I'm using this drill, players simply go too fast. To ensure that the pause is long enough at each cone, instruct the player to look at the wrist at each stop as if they were wearing a watch. Have the player verbally count to two before exploding to the next cone.

FULL-COURT ONE-ON-ONE DRILL

Setup

- Use two players, one basketball, and five cones.
- Player 1 is on offense and player 2 is on defense. Player 1 starts on the baseline with player 2 closely defending.

Execution

1. Player 1 must stay inbounds and not cross the midline of the court (the imaginary line running from rim to rim).

2. Player 1 works to advance the ball up the court to the cone placed on the wing on the opposite side.

3. Once player 1 reaches the cone, they must take two retreat dribbles (figure 1.17).

4. From here, player 1 and player 2 play one-on-one. If player 1 scores, then they keep possession of the basketball.

5. If player 1 does not score, then player 2 takes possession and switches court sides.

6. Players are awarded 1 point for every made basket.

7. The drill ends when one player has 7 points.

Coaching Point

Have players use the separation and positioning techniques to maintain inside position.

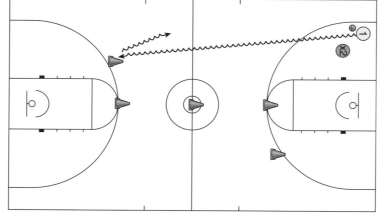

Figure 1.17 Full-court one-on-one drill.

FULL-COURT ZIGZAG DRILL

Refinement

Setup

- Use one basketball and one player.
- The player starts on the baseline with the ball.

Execution

1. The player takes two dribbles to the right, changes direction, and takes two dribbles to the left and changes direction. The player repeats this pattern until they reach the opposite baseline. The player can use any of the four change-of-direction moves (figure 1.18).

2. The player then continues the drill back to the baseline.

3. The player receives 1 point each time they change directions.

4. The player performs the drill for one minute.

5. Record the player's score.

Coaching Point

Players should keep their eyes up and focused on the middle of the floor and not on the particular direction that they are going.

Scorecard

Junior varsity: 10 to 16 changes of direction

Varsity: 17 to 23 changes of direction

All-conference: 24 to 30 changes of direction

All-American: 31 or more changes of direction

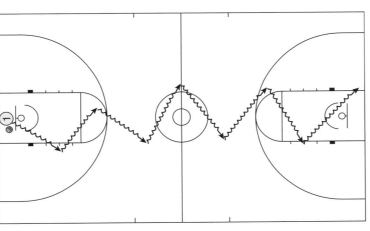

Figure 1.18 Full-court zigzag drill.

JOHN STOCKTON DRILL

Refinement

Setup

- Use one basketball, one player, and one tennis ball.
- The player is in a low and athletic stance with one basketball and one tennis ball.

Execution: Crossover

1. The player dribbles the basketball with one hand and tosses the tennis ball high into the air with the other.

2. While the tennis ball is in the air, the player executes as many crossover dribbles as possible; then the player catches the tennis ball.

3. If the player has trouble catching the tennis ball in the air, they can catch it on the first bounce.

4. The player receives 1 point for every crossover dribble executed while the tennis ball is in the air.

5. If the player drops the tennis ball or loses the dribble, the repetition does not count.

6. The player performs the drill for two minutes and records the best score.

Scorecard

Junior varsity: 1 to 2 points

Varsity: 3 to 4 points

All-conference: 5 to 6 points

All-American: 7 or more points

Execution: Between the Legs

1. The player dribbles the basketball with one hand and tosses the tennis ball high into the air with the other.

2. While the tennis ball is in the air, the player executes as many between-the-legs dribbles as possible; then the player catches the tennis ball.

3. If the player has trouble catching the tennis ball in the air, they can catch it on the first bounce.

4. The player receives 1 point for every between-the-legs dribble executed while the tennis ball is in the air.

5. If the player drops the tennis ball or loses the dribble, the repetition does not count.

6. The player performs the drill for two minutes and records the best score.

Scorecard

Junior varsity: 1 to 2 points

Varsity: 3 to 4 points

All-conference: 5 to 6 points

All-American: 7 or more points

Execution: Behind the Back

1. The player dribbles the basketball with one hand and tosses the tennis ball high into the air with the other.

2. While the tennis ball is in the air, the player executes as many behind-the-back dribbles as possible; then the player catches the tennis ball.

3. If the player has trouble catching the tennis ball in the air, they can catch it on the first bounce.

4. The player receives 1 point for every behind-the-back dribble executed while the tennis ball is in the air.

5. If the player drops the tennis ball or loses the dribble, the repetition does not count.

6. The player performs the drill for two minutes and records the best score.

Scorecard

Junior varsity: 1 to 2 points

Varsity: 3 to 4 points

All-conference: 5 to 6 points

All-American: 7 or more points

Coaching Point

This drill takes away all sight of the basketball and is one of my favorites to build court vision.

TENNIS BALL SNATCHES DRILLS

Setup

- Use one player, one basketball, and one tennis ball.
- The player begins in a low and athletic stance.

Execution: Pounds

1. The player pounds the dribble with one hand while tossing and then snatching a tennis ball (palm down) with the opposite hand.

2. If the player has trouble snatching the tennis ball in the air, they can snatch it on the first bounce.

3. The player receives 1 point each time they successfully snatch the tennis ball while maintaining the dribble with the opposite hand.

4. If they lose the dribble or drop the tennis ball, the repetition does not count.

5. The player performs the drill for 30 seconds with each hand and records each score.

Scorecard

Junior varsity: 5 to 10 snatches

Varsity: 11 to 20 snatches

All-conference: 21 to 30 snatches

All-American: 31 or more snatches

Execution: Crossover

1. The player pounds the dribble with one hand while tossing the tennis ball in the air with the opposite hand.

2. While the tennis ball is in the air, the player crosses the basketball quickly from one hand to the other and snatches the tennis ball (palm down) with the free hand, then repeats the move.

3. If the player has trouble snatching the tennis ball in the air, they can snatch it on the first bounce.

4. The player receives 1 point each time they successfully snatch the tennis ball after completing a crossover dribble.

5. If the player loses the dribble, doesn't complete the crossover, or drops the tennis ball, the repetition does not count.

6. The player performs the drill for 30 seconds and records the score.

Scorecard

Junior varsity: 5 to 10 snatches

Varsity: 11 to 20 snatches

All-conference: 21 to 30 snatches

All-American: 31 or more snatches

Execution: Between the Legs

1. The player pounds the basketball with one hand while tossing the tennis ball in the air with the opposite hand.

2. While the tennis ball is in the air, the player quickly executes a between-the-legs dribble from one hand to the other and snatches the tennis ball (palm down) with the free hand.

3. If the player has trouble snatching the tennis ball in the air, they can snatch it on the first bounce.

4. The player receives 1 point each time they successfully complete a between-the-legs dribble and then snatch the tennis ball.

5. If the player loses the dribble, doesn't complete the between-the-legs dribble, or drops the tennis ball, the repetition does not count.

6. The player performs the drill for 30 seconds and records the score.

Scorecard

Junior varsity: 5 to 10 snatches

Varsity: 11 to 20 snatches

All-conference: 21 to 30 snatches

All-American: 31 or more snatches

Execution: Behind the Back

1. The player pounds the dribble with one hand while tossing the tennis ball in the air with the opposite hand.

2. While the tennis ball is in the air, the player quickly executes a behind-the-back dribble from one hand to the other and snatches the tennis ball (palm down) with the free hand.

3. If the player has trouble snatching the tennis ball in the air, they can snatch it on the first bounce.

4. The player receives 1 point each time they successfully complete a behind-the-back dribble and then snatch the tennis ball.

5. If the player loses the dribble, doesn't complete the behind-the-back dribble, or drops the tennis ball, the repetition does not count.

6. The player performs the drill for 30 seconds and records the score.

Scorecard

Junior varsity: 5 to 10 catches

Varsity: 11 to 20 catches

All-conference: 21 to 30 catches

All-American: 31 or more catches

Coaching Point

These drills are used to develop off-hand ball protection as well as coordination, comfort, and confidence with the basketball.

TWO-BALL STATIONARY DRILLS

Refinement

Setup

- Use one player and two basketballs.
- The player begins in a low and athletic stance with both balls.

Execution: Two-Ball Same

1. The player simultaneously pounds both basketballs at knee level.
2. The player receives 1 point for every successful dribble.
3. The player performs the drill for 30 seconds and records the score.

Scorecard

Junior varsity: 10 to 15 dribbles

Varsity: 16 to 25 dribbles

All-conference: 26 to 35 dribbles

All-American: 35 or more dribbles

Execution: Two-Ball Alternate

1. The player pounds both basketballs in an alternating pattern at knee level.
2. The player receives 1 point for every successful dribble.
3. The player performs the drill for 30 seconds and records the score.

Scorecard

Junior varsity: 20 to 25 dribbles

Varsity: 26 to 35 dribbles

All-conference: 36 to 45 dribbles

All-American: 46 or more dribbles

Execution: Two-Ball Crossover

1. The player pounds both basketballs simultaneously for two repetitions and then crosses each ball to the opposite hand.
2. The player receives 1 point each time they complete a two-ball crossover.
3. The player performs the drill for 30 seconds and records the score.

Scorecard

Junior varsity: 5 to 10 crossovers

Varsity: 11 to 15 crossovers

All-conference: 16 to 20 crossovers

All-American: 21 or more crossovers

Execution: Two-Ball Between the Legs

1. The player pounds both basketballs simultaneously for two repetitions and then executes a between-the-legs dribble and exchanges the other ball to the opposite hand with a crossover dribble.

2. The player receives 1 point each time they complete a two-ball between-the-legs dribble.

3. The player performs the drill for 30 seconds and records the score.

Scorecard

Junior varsity: 5 to 10 between-the-legs dribbles

Varsity: 11 to 15 between-the-legs dribbles

All-conference: 16 to 20 between-the-legs dribbles

All-American: 21 or more between-the-legs dribbles

Execution: Two-Ball Behind the Back

1. The player pounds both basketballs simultaneously for two repetitions and then executes a behind-the-back dribble with one ball and exchanges the other ball to the opposite hand with a crossover dribble.

2. The player receives 1 point each time they complete a two-ball behind-the-back dribble.

3. The player performs the drill for 30 seconds and records the score.

Scorecard

Junior varsity: 5 to 10 behind-the-back dribbles

Varsity: 11 to 15 behind-the-back dribbles

All-conference: 16 to 20 behind-the-back dribbles

All-American: 21 or more behind-the-back dribbles

Coaching Point

Training with two basketballs allows the player to train both hands at the same time, which will save time in the gym. In addition, it pushes the player outside of their comfort zone, which develops confidence. If you can handle two basketballs, then you can dominate with one.

STEPHEN CURRY SEPARATION ONE-ON-ONE DRILL

Setup

- Use two players and one basketball.

Execution

1. Players start a one-on-one game at half-court; player 2 closely defends.
2. Player 1 is limited to three dribbles and one shot to score.
3. If player 1 scores, they remain on offense.
4. If player 1 does not score, player 2 is now on offense and player 1 is on defense.
5. One point is awarded for every made basket.
6. The drill ends when one player scores 10 points.

Coaching Point

This is a great one-on-one drill that Stephen Curry showed me; it helps players use the dribble to separate. The player must go somewhere with the first dribble or shot selection will be extremely limited.

When I was a junior in college, I made a decision that I wanted to be one of the best ball handlers in the world. I spent four hours a day, six days a week, working solely on my dribbling skills. At the end of six months, I released a 10-minute video on YouTube showcasing my progress. That video subsequently went viral and launched my career as a basketball trainer. This was my introduction to the basketball world. Since then, my dribbling skills have opened many doors for me, and they have been a key to my success. If you master the ability to dribble the basketball, you'll open up driving opportunities and become a more valuable asset to your team.

Chapter 2

Passing

Hall of fame coach John Wooden once said, "It takes 10 hands to score a basket." This type of unselfish play helped him lead the University of California at Los Angeles to 10 national titles in 12 seasons from 1964 to 1975. Passing skills were the foundation of his program, as they are for any successful offensive team. Precision passing limits turnovers, improves field-goal percentages, and boosts team spirit. Good passing teams don't worry about who gets credit for scoring a basket or who makes the assist that leads to a made basket; they simply move the basketball with the purpose of gaining an advantageous position against the defense. In this chapter, I discuss the fundamentals for individual proficiency in passing and receiving the basketball as well as the concepts that are key to successful team passing.

PASSING 101

Good form and fundamentals are vital to passing success. Let's now review the proper mechanics of passing.

Elbows In

Keep your elbows at your sides and behind the basketball to ensure that your pass will go straight. A good shooter keeps the elbows in to ensure an accurate shot, and the same applies for making an on-target pass.

Feet for Balance

To ensure great balance and body control, take a small forward step and release your pass all in one motion. If you are right-handed, step with your right foot; if you are left-handed, step with your left foot. Balance and body control are key to keeping possession of the basketball by not committing a traveling violation or throwing an intercepted pass.

Straight-Line Passes

The quickest path between two points is a straight line. When making passes in the air, try to throw passes with speed that do not arc. Slow passes and arc passes get intercepted, whereas straight-line passes find the receivers. To make a straight-line pass, load and lock your elbows on your passes. Load the elbows and wrists into the body, and fire the pass away with an exaggerated extension of the elbows and a flick of the wrist as if you were punching the pass to your teammate. The elbows generate the power, and the wrists create backspin on the pass (see figure 2.1).

Figure 2.1 Straight-line pass.

Hit the Target

Passing requires great accuracy, whether you're making a penetrating pass into the heart of the defense or completing a pass to an open teammate's hands for a shot. Players that can throw on-target passes lower the risk of turnovers and improve shooting percentages. Too often at my camps, I see bad passes that lead to bad shots. It's important to throw quality passes, because the quality of the pass is correlated to the quality of the shot.

ON-TARGET PASSING DRILL

Breakdown

Setup

- Use two players and one basketball.
- Players stand on opposite sides of the lane, facing each other. Player 1 has the ball.

Execution

1. Player 2 gives player 1 a random passing target with the dominant hand and indicates which type of pass player 1 will make. (Players may work on any of the passes mentioned in this chapter.)
2. Player 1 must make an on-target pass and hit player 2's target hand.
3. Players perform the drill for one minute.

Coaching Point

Players should keep their eyes on the target and their elbows behind the basketball to ensure on-target passes.

Passing Lane

The passing lane is the space or angle an offensive player creates to more easily and accurately complete a pass against a defender. There are four passing lanes on the defender: two above each shoulder and two under each arm (see figure 2.2). Even the best defender can guard only two of these lanes at a given time. To be a good passer, you must master the art of deception to open these passing lanes. To beat the defender's hands and open a passing lane, remember to fake and go. Fake a pass to the right to complete a pass to the left, or fake a pass high to complete a pass low. A wise coach once said, "Fake a pass to make a pass."

Figure 2.2   Passing lane fake and go.

KEEP-AWAY DRILL

Breakdown

Setup

- Use three players and one basketball.
- Player 1 and player 2 line up on opposite sides of the lane and face each other. Player 3 defends.

Execution

1. Player 1 and player 2 complete passes to each other while player 3 defends.
2. Player 3 can defend only the offensive player who has the basketball.
3. If the offensive player commits a turnover or makes a pass that is deflected, that player must switch with player 3 and become the defender.
4. Players perform the drill for three minutes.

Coaching Point

In this drill, it is important for the offensive player to use the pivot to gain and maintain space for completing a successful pass.

TYPES OF PASSES

Different game situations require different passes for successful execution and delivery. An offensive player must learn, master, and know the purpose of the below fundamental passes to be effective. Let's now learn the how, when, and why behind each of the fundamental passes.

Chest Pass

The chest pass is likely the most-used pass in basketball. This pass is frequently used to advance the ball up the floor in transition, and it is also used to move the basketball quickly in the half-court setting when no one is between the passer and the receiver. To make a chest pass, hold the basketball tight to the chest with two hands. The elbows should be bent and tucked in to each side (figure 2.3a). Right-handed players step toward the receiver with the right foot, and left-handed players step with the left foot. Complete the pass all in one motion: step with the correct foot; exaggerate the extension of the elbows with a quick, explosive movement for power and flick the wrists; and finish with your palms facing outward to generate backspin (figure 2.3b). Hold the follow-through with the elbows extended, palms facing outward, fingers pointing toward the target, and thumbs pointing toward the ground.

Figure 2.3 Chest pass: (a) elbows in and (b) palms facing outward.

CHEST PASS DRILL

Breakdown

Setup

- Use one player and one basketball.
- Tape a 12-inch (30.5 cm) square to the wall at the height of the player's shoulders. The player stands about 15 feet (4.5 m) from the wall. (For all drills in which a ball is used against a wall, be sure to use a hard-surfaced wall.)

Execution

1. The player makes on-target chest passes, aiming for the inside of the square.

2. If the basketball does not hit the target, the repetition does not count.

3. Record the number of on-target chest passes made in one minute.

Coaching Point

Players should work at a high intensity and make sharp passes as if they are in game situations. Players should not make lazy passes.

Bounce Pass

The bounce pass is most commonly used to pass under the defense, such as getting the ball to a receiver who is cutting to the rim or getting the basketball into the post. When making a bounce pass, start in a triple-threat position and hold the basketball tight to the torso with two hands. The elbows should be bent and tucked in to each side. Right-handed players step toward the receiver with the right foot, and left-handed players step with the left foot. Complete the pass all in one motion: step with the correct foot; exaggerate the extension of the elbows with a quick, explosive movement for power and flick the wrists; and finish with your palms facing outward to generate backspin. Hold the follow-through with the elbows extended, palms facing outward, fingers pointing toward the target, and thumbs pointing toward the ground (see figure 2.4). Aim for a spot on the floor that is two-thirds of the distance to your receiver to ensure an on-time and on-target delivery.

BOUNCE PASS DRILL

Breakdown

Setup

- Use one player and one basketball.
- Tape a 12-inch (30.5 cm) square to the wall at the height of the player's waist. The player stands 15 feet (4.5 m) from the wall.

Execution

1. The player makes bounce passes, aiming for the inside of the square.
2. If the basketball does not hit the target, the repetition does not count.
3. Record the number of on-target bounce passes made in one minute.

Coaching Point

As previously mentioned, only sharp, direct-line passes should be made. If a player makes a soft or lazy pass and it hits the target, the repetition should not be counted.

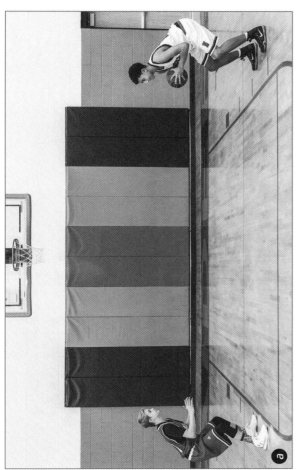

Figure 2.4 Bounce pass.

Overhead Pass

The third fundamental pass is the overhead pass. This is used to throw over an opponent or to make a long-distance pass, such as when starting a fast break with an outlet pass. To make an overhead pass, start in the triple-threat position with the basketball tight to the body for ball protection. Step toward your pass with the previously mentioned foot. Complete your pass all in one motion: Raise the basketball above the head; load the elbows and wrist, being careful not to overextend; and bring the basketball behind the head. On the release, extend the elbows violently, flick the wrists, and hold the follow-through with the palms facing outward, fingers pointing toward the target, and thumbs pointing toward the ground (see figure 2.5).

Figure 2.5 Overhead pass.

OVERHEAD PASS DRILL

Breakdown

Setup

- Use one player and one basketball.
- Tape a 12-inch (30.5 cm) square to the wall at the height of the player's shoulders. The player stands 15 feet (4.5 m) from the wall.

Execution

1. The player makes overhead passes, aiming for the inside of the square.
2. If the basketball does not hit the target, the repetition does not count.
3. Record the number of on-target overhead passes made in one minute.

Coaching Point

The player should not bring the basketball directly behind the head where it could be stolen in a game. It is called an overhead pass and not a behind-the-head pass for a reason!

Push Pass

The push pass is used most often to complete passes when you are being closely guarded. For example, it can be used to throw a penetrating pass, to reverse the basketball on the perimeter, or to beat a trap. The push pass allows the passer to shield the basketball while making a pass on either side of the body. The previously mentioned passes are all two-handed passes, whereas the push pass is made with one hand. Much like in a shot, the off hand in a push pass is used only for ball control and to guide the pass. Start with the basketball held firmly with two hands in a triple-threat position with the basketball positioned on the outside of the torso. While using the body to shield the basketball, step toward the receiver with either a direct step (a pass with the right hand while stepping with the right foot) or a crossover step (a pass with the right hand while stepping with the left foot). Release the pass all in one motion: Push the basketball with your outside hand, starting with the elbow bent and loaded behind the ball, and finishing with the elbow in full extension. Hold the follow-through with the palm facing outward, fingers pointing toward the target, and the thumb pointing toward the ground (see figure 2.6).

Figure 2.6 Push pass.

PUSH PASS DRILL

Breakdown

Setup

- Use one player and one basketball.
- Tape a 12-inch (30.5 cm) square to the wall at the height of the player's shoulders. The player stands 15 feet (4.5 m) from the wall.

Execution

1. The player completes one-hand push passes, aiming for the inside of the square.
2. If the basketball does not hit the target, the repetition does not count.
3. The player performs the drill for one minute with each hand.
4. Record the number of on-target one-hand push passes made with each hand in one minute.

Coaching Point

Be sure to work on the push pass using both the direct step and the crossover step.

THREE-PASS DRILL

Breakdown

Setup

- Use three players and three basketballs.
- Players stand 15 feet (4.5 m) apart in the shape of a triangle. Each player has a ball.

Execution

1. Each player makes a right-hand push pass to the right.
2. After catching the pass, each player makes another push pass to the right.
3. Players continue this pattern for 30 seconds.
4. After 30 seconds, players reverse the passing direction. Players now make left-hand push passes to the left for 30 seconds.
5. The goal of the drill is to complete 30 seconds of perfect passes with no dropped balls. If a player drops the ball, restart the clock. Players don't switch directions until they complete perfect passes for 30 seconds.

Coaching Point

This is a great way for players to perform a lot of passing repetitions in a team setting. I use it as a warm-up at many of my camps.

TEAM PASSING SUCCESS

Successful team passing requires patience, unselfishness, court awareness, and communication. A team that moves the basketball effectively will move the defense and create high-percentage scoring opportunities. Next, let's learn several important concepts that will improve team passing.

Penetrating Pass

A penetrating pass is any pass to a teammate that cuts through the first or second level of defense. The first level of defense is your defender; the second level of defense is your teammates' defenders. A pass to a teammate who is cutting to the rim on a give and go, a bounce pass to a post player on the low block, or a pass to a teammate on a back cut to the basket are all examples of penetrating passes. Penetrating passes often create scoring opportunities near the basket, more fouls, and more offensive rebounds. This is a great opportunity to seek out as a passer, but attempt it only if there is a high probability of completion. If you have doubts about completion, don't try to make a penetrating pass; simply move the basketball to your first open teammate.

Make the Easy Pass

You learn at a young age to share the basketball and pass to an open teammate. At my clinics, I like to take it a step further. I often see players trying to make what I call the "home-run pass." The home-run pass is a selfish, difficult pass that a player attempts to complete for a made basket. A player that tries to stuff the stat sheet by making home-run passes is not a team player, and this player can cause more harm than good. A good passer should try to make the easy pass or the single. A few easy passes can lead to an easy shot much the way a few singles in baseball can lead to scored runs. Throwing a single in basketball is simply passing to the first open teammate you see. Don't make passing more complex than it needs to be. Take it from legendary coach Bobby Knight, who said "Basketball is simple! Complete passes and you will win games!"

Make the Extra Pass

A phrase that I consistently hear when I'm around great passing teams is "one more!" They constantly try to make one more pass to find a better scoring opportunity. They pass up good shots in order to find great shots, and they quickly move the basketball from one player to another. The quicker an offensive team moves the basketball from one side of the floor to the other, the closer each defender will play, thus creating an opening in the lane for penetrating passes and dribble drives. Teams that are unselfish and strive to make the extra pass make themselves much harder to defend.

EXTRA PASS DRILL

Breakdown

Setup

- Use four or more players, one basketball, and four cones.
- The cones are placed at each wing, the top of the key, and the corner.

Execution

1. Player 1 begins the drill at cone 1 and completes a chest pass to player 2.

2. On making the pass, player 1 follows the pass and sprints to cone 2 while each player shouts "one more!"

3. After the catch, player 2 completes a chest pass to player 3.

4. On making the pass, player 2 follows the pass and sprints to cone 3 while each player shouts "one more!"

5. After the catch, player 3 completes a chest pass to player 4.

6. On making the pass, player 3 follows the pass and sprints to cone 4 while each player shouts "one more!"

7. After the catch, player 4 attacks the basket for a layup (figure 2.7).

8. After converting the layup, player 4 rebounds the shot and returns to cone 1 to repeat the drill.

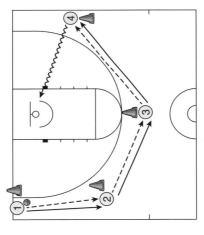

Figure 2.7 Extra pass drill.

Coaching Point

Making the extra pass is the key to breaking down a good defensive team.

CATCHING 101

Passing and catching go hand and hand. Next, I break down the fundamentals of being a good receiver.

Stance

Be ready for the next play by beginning in a prepared stance with your knees bent, back straight, and feet shoulder-width apart. The elbows are tucked in at each side, the palm of each hand faces the passer, and all 10 fingers point toward the ceiling (see figure 2.8).

Show Hands

It is important to give the passer a target by showing your hands. The best place to catch the basketball is on your shooting side at shoulder level; this position allows you to quickly transfer the basketball into a shot. As previously mentioned, the palm of each hand faces the passer and all 10 fingers are spread wide and point toward the ceiling.

Speak

You should always say three things to the passer: (1) the passer's name, (2) *ball* (say this in a strong and confident tone to demand the ball), and (3) your location on the court (e.g., "Carlos! Ball! At the elbow!"). Communicating will help the passer find you when it is most advantageous.

See

Maintain visual contact with the basketball until there is physical contact. Watch the flight of the basketball until it comes in contact with your hands. Most dropped passes occur because of a loss of visual contact.

Figure 2.8   Catching stance.

Absorb the Pass

To catch a high-speed pass, make sure your fingers are spread and your wrists and arms are flexible and ready to absorb the pass. It's vital that you give with the ball and bring it toward your body and that you not be stiff in your hands, wrists, and arms.

Meet the Pass

When you are closely guarded by an opponent, meet each pass with your hands and your feet. While the pass is in the air, sprint toward the ball with your hands outstretched. Always give up your position on the court to keep possession of the basketball. When you catch the basketball, bring it close to your body on your shooting side to secure and protect it.

See Before the Catch

The best passers know where they are going to pass the basketball before they ever receive it, and they try to think one play ahead of the defense. To have this special type of court vision, or as I call it, *psychic vision*, you must survey the court before you receive a pass. Take a quick glance at the rim or the middle of the floor just before you receive a pass; this will give you and your team a one-second advantage on the next play.

Receiver Checklist

What's your first priority when you catch the basketball? This is an important question. The following checklist shows you what steps you should take in order to find and create opportunities for the team.

1. Square your body to the rim and look for a scoring opportunity for yourself.

2. If there's not a shot for you, look toward the middle of the floor for an opportunity to make a penetrating pass into the lane for a likely shot by a teammate.

3. If a penetrating pass is not an option, quickly reverse the basketball around the perimeter to the first open teammate.

4. Follow this checklist to ensure that you don't miss any scoring opportunities.

CATCHING 101 DRILL

Breakdown

Setup

- Use two players, one basketball, and two cones.
- Players each stand next to a cone on opposite sides of the lane and face each other.

Execution

1. Player 1 starts with the basketball.
2. Player 2 must drop low, touch the cone, and remain in a low stance while showing their hands and calling for the basketball (figure 2.9a).
3. Player 1 passes the ball, and player 2 must meet the pass with the hands and feet (figure 2.9b).
4. When Player 2 catches the ball, player 1 must drop low, touch the cone, and remain in a low stance while showing their hands and calling for the basketball.
5. Player 2 passes the ball, and player 1 must meet the pass with the hands and feet.
6. Players perform the drill for one minute.

Coaching Point

Players should keep visual contact with the ball until there is physical contact.

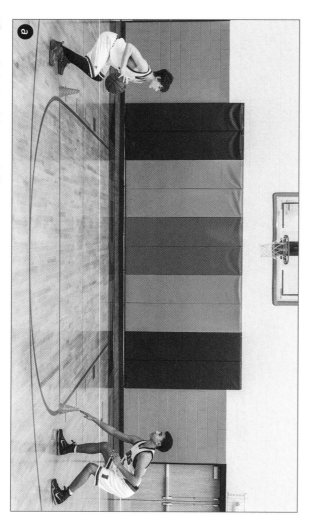

Figure 2.9   Catching 101 drill.

a

Figure 2.9 *(continued)* Catching 101 drill.

Triple Threat

When you receive a pass, use the triple-threat stance in order to be a more efficient and effective offensive player. From this position, you can quickly pass, shoot, or dribble. To enter this position, square your body to the rim and maintain a low and athletic stance with the knees bent, the feet shoulder-width apart, and your weight on the balls of the feet. Hold the ball with two hands tight to the body on the shooting side and tuck the shooting elbow under the ball (see figure 2.10). The farther the basketball is from the body, the weaker you will be. Keep the basketball close to the body and bend your elbows for greater strength and ball security. Your eyes should be focused on the area around the rim rather than in one particular direction or on a teammate; this allows you to efficiently see the entire floor with your peripheral vision, which increases your options.

Figure 2.10 Triple-threat stance.

REFINEMENT DRILLS

You now have a firm understanding of individual passing and catching fundamentals as well as how to break down the defense with the pass in the team setting. Now it's time to elevate your skills with refinement drills. This is where the real training begins!

CONE PASSING DRILL

Refinement

Setup

- Use two players, one basketball, and one cone.
- Player 1 has the basketball at the top of the key. Player 2 stands behind a cone that is placed on the low block.

Execution

1. Player 1 must stay behind the three-point line, complete a two-hand bounce pass at the cone, and then run to the free-throw line (figure 2.11).

2. If the basketball knocks the cone over, player 1 receives a point.

3. After the pass, player 2 retrieves the basketball and passes it back to player 1, who then takes a shot near the free-throw line.

4. If player 1 makes the shot, an additional point is awarded.

5. No points are given for missed shots or for inaccurate passes that do not strike the cone.

6. After player 1's shot attempt, it is player 2's turn. Player 2 repeats the previous steps.

7. Players complete the drill for five minutes and remember their scores.

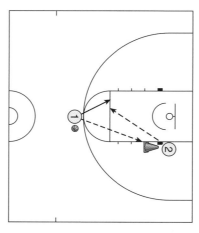

Figure 2.11 Cone passing drill.

Coaching Point

If you want to elevate the drill, add a second basketball; this forces the passer to make accurate passes with one hand. In this progression, the offensive player starts the drill outside the three point arc with two basketballs. Player 1 must make a one hand pass to the cone with one basketball and then dribble the remaining basketball to the free throw line for a shot attempt.

PASSING TAG DRILL

Refinement

Setup

- Use two teams of five players and one basketball.
- The clock starts when the offensive team makes their first pass.

Execution

The goal of the drill is to pass, move, and communicate in an attempt to tag one of the opposing team's players with the basketball (figure 2.12).

1. The offense is not allowed to dribble; they may only pass and pivot.

2. The opposing team is not allowed to touch the basketball, and they should try to evade it while staying inbounds.

3. When a player is tagged or goes outside the baseline, sideline, or half-court boundary, that player is out.

4. The possession ends when all five players have been tagged out. Stop the clock and record the time.

5. The opposing team then gains offensive possession and repeats the drill.

6. The team with the shortest time wins.

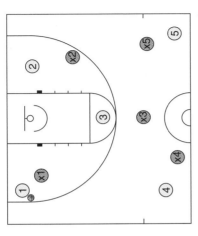

Figure 2.12   Passing tag drill.

Coaching Point

This is a great drill to teach teamwork and communication. If the players do not speak and do not work together, there is little chance of success in this drill.

SPEED PASSING DRILL

Refinement

Setup

- Use two players and two basketballs.
- Players start on opposite sides of the lane and face each other; each player has a ball.

Execution

1. Players each make a right-hand push pass and then quickly make another.
2. The goal of the drill is to be fast enough to put two basketballs in the other player's hands at one time. If this happens, or if one player drops the pass, the game ends.
3. Players complete the drill with the right hand and the left hand.

Coaching Point

This is a great drill to get your players to work at a high intensity and to put stress on their passing and catching skills. If you stress these skills, they will improve.

50-POINT DRILL

Refinement

Setup

- Use two teams of five players and one basketball.
- The game is played in the half-court.

Execution

1. Offensive players are not allowed to dribble; they can only pass and pivot (figure 2.13).

2. Defensive players must defend man to man with no trapping.

3. Points are accumulated by completing passes. The offensive team receives 1 point for every completed pass. The offensive team can also receive points by converting on a shot.

4. The offensive team receives 10 points for every made shot and also retains possession of the basketball.

5. If the defense causes a turnover or creates a deflection, or if the offense commits a dribbling violation, possession of the ball immediately changes but the offense keeps the points they have accumulated thus far.

6. If the offensive team misses a shot, possession of the basketball changes and they lose their accumulated points.

7. The game ends when one team has 50 points.

Figure 2.13 50-point drill.

Coaching Point

The purpose of this drill is to teach ball toughness, movement without the basketball, and shot selection. Oftentimes, the competitiveness of the drill will bring out the assistant coach in each of your players as ill-advised shots are taken and careless turnovers are made. This is one of my favorite team passing drills!

THREE-PASS DRILL

Setup

- Use three players and three basketballs.
- Players stand 15 feet (4.5 m) apart in the shape of a triangle. Each player has a ball.

Execution

1. Each player makes a right-hand push pass to the right (figure 2.14).

2. After catching the pass, each player makes another push pass to the right.

3. Players continue in this pattern for 30 seconds.

4. After 30 seconds, players reverse the passing direction. Players now make left-hand push passes to the left for 30 seconds.

5. The goal of the drill is to complete 30 seconds of perfect passes with no dropped balls. If a player drops the ball, restart the clock. Players don't switch directions until they complete perfect passes for 30 seconds.

Figure 2.14 Three-pass drill.

Coaching Point

In the game, the quicker the basketball moves from one side of the floor to the other, the closer players will defend. This is a very useful drill for getting players in the habit of passing the ball quickly. In addition, it focuses on passing and catching skills.

ULTIMATE BASKETBALL DRILL

Refinement

Setup

- Use two teams of five players and one basketball.
- The game is played using the full court.

Execution

1. Offensive players are not allowed to dribble the ball; they can only pass and pivot to advance the ball up the court. They must also respect the sideline boundaries (figure 2.15).

2. Defensive players must defend man to man with no trapping.

3. If there's a turnover, deflection, or dropped pass, possession of the basketball immediately changes.

4. The goal of the game is to complete a pass into the end zone. The end zone is the out-of-bounds area at either baseline.

5. If a pass is completed in the end zone, the offensive team receives 1 point and the possession changes.

6. Players perform the drill for 10 minutes. The team with the highest number of points at the end wins.

Coaching Point

Your players will love this drill! It has always been a player favorite at my camps, and it has so many useful teaching moments for you to stop the action and instruct.

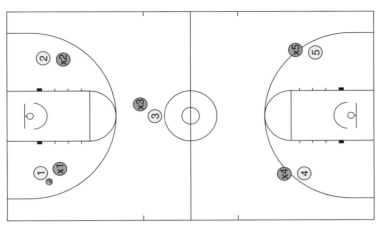

Figure 2.15 Ultimate basketball drill.

Passing is crucial to a team's offensive success. Former NBA star Jason Williams said that while growing up in West Virginia, he had a key to his local gym and he routinely trained for hours and would never take a shot. Instead, he worked on passing the basketball off the wall in every conceivable way. Jason had a passion for passing, and it helped him become an NBA champion in 2006. Learn from Jason Williams and grab a ball, find a wall, and begin to use your imagination. Put yourself in a game situation and work on applicable passes at game speed against the wall until you master them. If you develop a passion for passing, you and your team will improve.

Chapter 3

Inside Shots

Shooting near basket is a neglected and undertaught skill. Even though the layup is the highest-percentage shot in basketball, many shots are still routinely missed at or near the rim. How can this basic shot that is so close to the basket ever be missed? The best answer is that an inside shot that is highly contested by the defense is not a simple shot. In fact, it's a shot that requires great skill. Players consistently, but reluctantly, take highly contested layups and finishes near the rim. Why do they take these higher skill and lower accuracy inside shots? They don't understand how to open a scoring window through which to finish. In this chapter, I discuss fundamentals and offensive maneuvers that you can use to open these windows and find success with inside shots. I break down these skills in one-player drills for understanding and retention, and then I refine these skills through a series of one-on-one drills for game success. Let's get started, so you can learn to finish!

FINISHING FUNDAMENTALS

One of the worst feelings in basketball is when you execute a flashy, billion-dollar move with precision and then follow it up with a 25-cent finish by missing the easy shot at or near the basket. In this section, I outline the techniques necessary for success with inside shots so this doesn't happen to you!

Body and Ball Control

Control your body, but don't let your body control you! The ability to be on balance and to control your body is important for inside shots. Finishing near the basket may require sudden changes of direction, rapid decelerations, quick pivots, bodily contact, and collisions. Maintain a low and athletic stance and put your weight on the balls of your feet to ensure body control. To ensure ball control, always finish with two hands on the basketball. Control the ball, but don't let the ball control you!

Eyes on the Basket

To be an effective finisher near the basket, your eyes must be locked on the basket from the beginning of the shot until the basketball drops through the bottom of the net. Players tend to focus on the defense and lose sight of the hoop, but this can lower your field-goal percentage. Ignore the distractions and keep a laser focus on the target.

Use Your Shield

You will learn numerous inside shots and maneuvers in this chapter, but one common fundamental each is the use of the shield. It is imperative that you keep your body between the defender and the basketball. Create a barrier that prevents your shooting hand or the basketball from being touched.

Build Ambidexterity

The ability to finish with the right or the left hand is of utmost importance, but it takes tremendous persistence and patience to master this. To be proficient, you must be able to finish effectively with either hand within 10 feet of the rim. Ambidexterity allows you to shield the basketball and create space from the defense at all times, thus opening a scoring window. Shielding the basketball with your body and finding space are requirements for anyone seeking success with inside shots.

Backboard Square

The square on the backboard is a great tool to use when shooting a layup or an inside shot, but you must know where to aim. The square on the backboard can be broken down into four quadrants. When shooting an inside shot or a layup from the wing, it is most effective to aim for quadrant 3 or 4. When attempting a shot in front of the rim, where the angle makes it tougher to use the square, it is more accurate to shoot without using the square. See figure 3.1 for clarification on where to aim based on the angle of your shot.

The Scoring Window

The scoring window is the space or angle an offensive player creates to more easily and accurately score an inside shot against the defender. You can open the scoring window in various ways, such as mastering ambidexterity in your

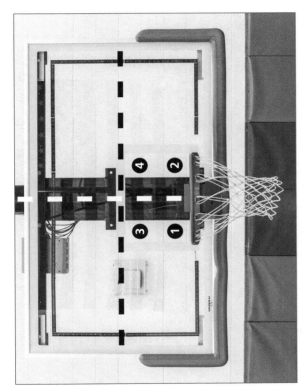

Figure 3.1 Backboard square.

finish, making correct reads and reactions to defense, shielding the basketball from the defense with your body, and using great footwork and finishing maneuvers. In the next section, you will learn how to open the scoring window in very common defensive scenarios.

TYPES OF LAYUPS

The layup is one of the highest-percentage shots in basketball; it is second only to the dunk. Proper finishing fundamentals are important in this low skill, high-accuracy inside shot. Let's review several of the most common layups.

Inside-Foot Layup

The inside-foot layup is a type of finish used when the defender is between the offensive player and the basket. In this scenario, jump off the inside foot and finish the shot with the outside hand, using the body as a shield to protect the basketball. A good offensive player always protects the ball with the off hand and body to create a better scoring window. Review the break-down drills to build an understanding of and comfort with the inside-foot layup.

After picking up the dribble, take two steps. The first step is with the outside foot and the second step is with the inside foot. The first step is long and the second is short in order to maintain body control. Land on the second step in a low and athletic position; then launch up and toward the basket and protect the basketball on the outside of the body by finishing with an outside-hand layup off the correct quadrant. During this maneuver, focus on the basket until the basketball comes through the bottom of the net (see figure 3.2).

Figure 3.2 Inside-foot layup.

INSIDE-FOOT LAYUP CHOREOGRAPHY DRILL

Breakdown

Setup

- Use one player and one basketball.
- The player is on the baseline with the ball.

Execution

1. The player gets into a low and athletic stance by bending down and touching the basketball to the ground.

2. The player then takes two steps to the right without a dribble. The first step (with the right foot) is long and the second step (with the left foot) is short.

3. The player then explodes off the ground and shoots a right-hand layup straight up in the air.

4. The player then catches the ball and returns to a low and athletic stance by bending down and touching the basketball to the ground.

5. The player continues by taking two steps to the left without a dribble. The first step (with the left foot) is long and the second step (with the right foot) is short.

6. The player then explodes off the ground and shoots a left-hand layup straight up in the air.

7. The player repeats these steps in a zigzag motion and stops at the opposite baseline.

INSIDE-FOOT LAYUP CONE DRILL

Breakdown

Setup

- Use one player, one basketball, and one cone.
- The player has the ball and stands at the cone, which is placed just above the block.

Execution

1. The player gets into a low and athletic stance by bending down and touching the basketball to the floor.

2. The player takes two steps toward the rim: a long step with the outside foot followed by a short step with the inside foot.

3. The player then jumps up toward the basket and finishes with a layup off the backboard with the outside hand.

4. The player repeats these steps on both sides of the basket and completes 10 layups with each hand.

INSIDE-FOOT LAYUP GAME-READY DRILL

Breakdown

Setup

- Use one player, one basketball, and six cones.
- The player stands under the rim with the basketball.

Execution

1. The player dribbles inside and around cone 1.

2. The player then faces the basket and attacks the rim by dribbling through cones 2 and 3 with the outside hand, which creates the perfect angle for the player to finish at the rim with an inside-foot layup off the backboard (figure 3.3).

3. The player rebounds the shot and dribbles inside and around cone 1 on the opposite side of the court.

4. The player then faces the basket and attacks the rim by dribbling through cones 2 and 3 with the outside hand, which again creates the perfect angle for the player to finish at the rim with an inside-foot layup off the backboard.

5. The player repeats the drill until 10 layups are made with correct form.

Coaching Point

A player should keep the eyes on the ball from the beginning of the shot until it comes through the bottom of the net.

Figure 3.3 Inside-foot layup game-ready drill.

Outside-Foot Layup

When I watch youth basketball practices, I am confused when coaches use only the inside-foot layup. There are many situations in the game that call for alternate finishes at the rim. The inside-foot layup is appropriate only when the defender occupies the inside position between the offensive player and the basket. Sometimes the offensive player may be between the defender and the basket; in this scenario, the offensive player may need to finish with the inside hand and jump off the outside foot to protect and shield the basketball from the defender and to open a scoring window.

After picking up the dribble, take two steps. The first step is with the inside foot and the second step is with the outside foot. The first step is long and the second is short in order to maintain body control. Land on the second step in a low and athletic position; then launch up and toward the basket and protect the basketball on the inside of the body by finishing with an inside-hand layup off the correct quadrant. During this maneuver, focus on the basket until the basketball comes through the bottom of the net (see figure 3.4).

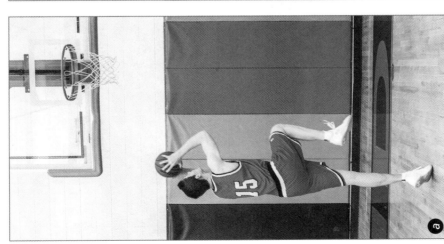
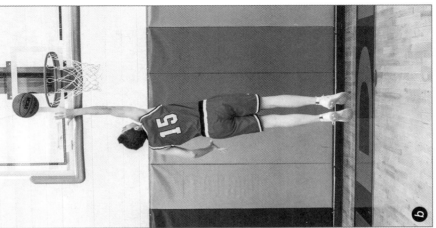

Figure 3.4 Outside-foot layup.

OUTSIDE-FOOT LAYUP CHOREOGRAPHY DRILL

Breakdown

Setup

- Use one player and one basketball.
- The player is on the baseline with the ball.

Execution

1. The player gets into a low and athletic stance by bending down and touching the basketball to the ground.

2. The player then takes two steps to the right without a dribble. The first step (with the left foot) is long and the second step (with the right foot) is short.

3. The player then explodes off the ground and shoots a left-hand layup straight up in the air.

4. The player then catches the ball and returns to a low and athletic stance by bending down and touching the basketball to the ground.

5. The player continues by taking two steps to the left without a dribble. The first step (with the right foot) is long and the second step (with the left foot) is short.

6. The player then explodes off the ground and shoots a right-hand layup straight up in air.

7. The player repeats these steps in a zigzag motion and stops at the opposite baseline.

OUTSIDE-FOOT LAYUP CONE DRILL

Breakdown

Setup

- One player, one basketball, and one cone.
- The player has the ball and stands at the cone, which is placed just above the block.

Execution

1. The player gets into a low and athletic stance by bending down and touching the basketball to the floor.

2. The player takes two steps toward the rim: a long step with the inside foot followed by a short step with the outside foot.

3. The player then jumps up toward the basket and finishes with a layup off the backboard with the inside hand.

4. The player repeats these steps on both sides of the basket and completes 10 layups with each hand.

OUTSIDE-FOOT LAYUP GAME-READY DRILL

Breakdown

Setup

- Use one player, one ball, and six cones.
- The player stands under the rim with the basketball.

Execution

1. The player dribbles inside and around cone 1.

2. The player then faces the basket and attacks the rim by dribbling through cones 2 and 3 with the outside hand, which creates the perfect angle for the player to finish at the rim with an outside-foot layup off the backboard (figure 3.5).

3. The player rebounds the shot and dribbles inside and around cone 1 on the opposite side of the court.

4. The player then faces the basket and attacks the rim by dribbling through cones 2 and 3 with the outside hand, which again creates the perfect angle for the player to finish at the rim with an outside-foot layup off the backboard.

5. The player repeats the drill until 10 layups are made with correct form.

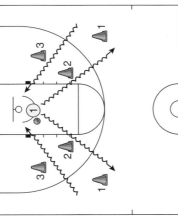

Figure 3.5 Outside-foot layup game-ready drill.

Coaching Point

The player should protect the ball with the outside shoulder to prevent a deflection from the defender.

Power Layup

The third type of layup is the power layup. More fouls occur on inside shots than on any other type of shot. The power layup is most often used when an offensive player is being closely defended and physical contact, collisions, and fouls are likely. The previously discussed layups are shot on one foot, but the power layup is shot on two feet. The power layup allows the offense to finish with strength, balance, and control.

When picking up the dribble or catching a pass or rebound, leap off the ground using both feet and land squarely in a low and athletic stance on two feet with your toes and shoulders pointed toward the baseline. When you land, launch

up and toward the basket for a two-foot power layup off the correct quadrant. Protect the basketball from the defender by using your body as a shield between the defense and the basketball. During this maneuver, focus on the basket until the basketball comes through the bottom of the net (see figure 3.6).

Figure 3.6 Power layup.

POWER LAYUP CONE DRILL

Breakdown

Setup

- Use one player, one basketball, and one cone.
- The player stands at the cone with the ball.

Execution

1. The player gently tosses the basketball off the backboard.

2. The player then jumps and catches the basketball in the air and lands on two feet with a low and wide base and with the toes and shoulders pointed toward the baseline.

3. The player reinforces a low and athletic stance by bending at the knees and touching the basketball to the ground.

4. From here the player jumps high with two feet and finishes with a power layup with the outside hand (figure 3.7).

5. The player repeats these steps on each side of the basket until 10 power layups are made.

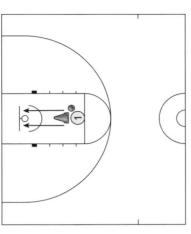

Figure 3.7 Power layup cone drill.

POWER LAYUP GAME-READY DRILL

Setup

- Use one player, one basketball, and one cone.
- The player stands under the rim with the ball. The cone is placed at the top of the key.

Execution

1. The player dribbles to the cone and touches it.

2. The player then attacks either the left or the right side of the basket and comes to a one- or two-brake on-balance stop with a low and wide base and with the toes and shoulders pointed toward the baseline.

3. The player jumps high and shoots with an outside-hand power layup (figure 3.8).

4. The player completes five power layups on each side of the basket.

Coaching Point

The best time to use the power layup in the game is when the defense is close or is in contact with a player. The power layup will help players own the space they're in and finish through physical contact while maintaining balance and body control.

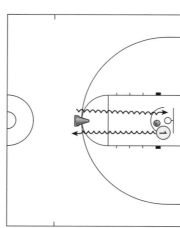

Figure 3.8   Power layup game-ready drill.

FINISHING FOOTWORK MANEUVERS

I heard a wise coach say "Basketball is a game where your feet will put you into a position to use your hands." This is true when you are trying to create a better scoring window on an inside shot.

Inside Pivot

The inside pivot is a footwork maneuver that is most commonly used when the defender cuts off your path to the basket or when the defender's hands are high. You can react by pivoting on the inside foot and stepping across the body and the feet of the defender with the outside foot. By beating the defender's feet, you create a scoring window through which you can more easily and accurately finish.

When the defender is too close, their hands are high, or they cut off your path to the basket, use the inside pivot. Starting in a low and athletic stance with your body between the defender and the basketball, plant your inside foot to the floor and pivot by stepping across your body and the defender's body with the outside foot. The goal is to get your foot, the basketball, and your shoulders past the defender. From here, maintain a low and athletic stance and jump high for the shot with two feet. Your momentum should be toward the rim. Make the shot with the outside hand for a shielded finish (see figure 3.9).

Figure 3.9   Inside pivot.

INSIDE PIVOT CHOREOGRAPHY DRILL

Breakdown

Setup

- Use one player, one basketball, and two cones.
- The cones are placed on the left and right sides of the basket. The player has the ball and stands on the outside of one of the cones.

Execution

1. The player gets in a low and athletic stance with the feet squared by bending at the knees and touching the basketball to the floor.

2. The player demonstrates an inside pivot finish by keeping the inside foot planted and taking a long step across the body with the outside foot to the inside of the lane.

3. The player completes the move by jumping with two feet and taking a shielded outside-hand shot (figure 3.10).

4. The player completes the choreography five times on each side of the basket.

Figure 3.10 Inside pivot choreography drill.

INSIDE PIVOT GAME-READY DRILL

Breakdown

Setup

- Use one player, one basketball, and four cones.
- The player has the ball on the baseline on the lane line extended on either the right or the left side of the basket.

Execution

1. The player gets in a low and athletic stance with the feet squared by bending at the knees and touching the basketball to the floor.

2. The player then takes two dribbles to the outside of cone 1 and arrives with a two-brake stop with the inside foot first and the outside foot second.

3. The player demonstrates an inside pivot finish by keeping the inside foot planted and taking a long step across the body with the outside foot to the inside of the lane.

4. The player completes the maneuver by jumping with two feet and taking a shielded outside-hand shot straight up in the air and not at the basket.

5. The player repeats the choreography at cones 2, 3, and 4 (figure 3.11).

6. At cone 4, the player finishes the choreography by taking a shot at the basket.

7. The player completes the drill five times on each side of the basket.

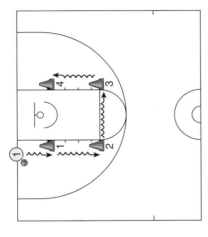

Figure 3.11 Inside pivot game-ready drill.

Coaching Point

To avoid a traveling violation when using the inside pivot maneuver, instruct your players to jump with two feet when taking the inside shot. A good way to help them remember this is to say "step through and jump off two."

Outside Pivot

The outside pivot is another footwork maneuver that alleviates pressure from the defense and creates space. It is used when the defensive player overextends and tries to block the offensive player's shot attempt. The offensive player can react by planting the outside foot firmly to the ground and taking a long forward step with the inside foot while simultaneously lifting the basketball up into a shot fake. When the defense is engaged, the offensive player quickly pivots away from the basket on the outside foot. This pivot will create space from the defense and provide a scoring window through which to finish.

When the defender overextends on your drive and tries to block your shot attempt, use the outside pivot. Plant the outside foot firmly to the ground and take a long forward step with the inside foot while simultaneously extending the basketball toward the basket with two hands for a shot fake. While maintaining a low stance, pivot away from the basket on the outside foot until the inside shoulder is pointing toward the rim. From here, jump high for the shot, making sure to shoot with the outside hand to shield the basketball from the defense (see figure 3.12).

Figure 3.12 Outside pivot.

OUTSIDE PIVOT CHOREOGRAPHY DRILL

Breakdown

Setup

- Use one player, one basketball, and two cones.
- The cones are placed on the left and right sides of the basket. The player has the ball and stands on the outside of one of the cones.

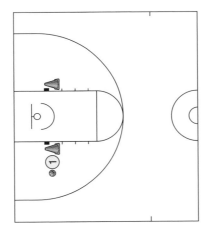

Figure 3.13 Outside pivot choreography drill.

Execution

1. The player gets in a low and athletic stance with the feet squared by bending at the knees and touching the basketball to the floor.

2. The player demonstrates an outside pivot inside shot by taking a long and extended step with the inside foot while simultaneously extending the basketball toward the rim for a shot fake.

3. The player then pivots away from the basket on the outside foot until the inside shoulder points to the rim.

4. The player completes the move by jumping high and taking a shielded outside-hand shot (figure 3.13).

5. The player completes the choreography five times on each side of the basket.

OUTSIDE PIVOT GAME-READY DRILL

Breakdown

Setup

- Use one player, one basketball, and four cones, as shown in the diagram. The player has the ball on the baseline of the lane line extended on either the right or the left side of the basket.

Execution

1. The player gets in a low and athletic stance with the feet squared by bending at the knees and touching the basketball to the floor.

2. The player demonstrates an outside pivot inside shot by taking two dribbles to the outside of cone 1, planting the outside foot first, and making a long and extended step with the inside foot while simultaneously extending the basketball outward for a shot fake.

3. The player then pivots away on the outside foot and finishes by taking a shielded outside-hand shot straight up in the air.

4. The player repeats the choreography at cones 2, 3, and 4 (figure 3.14).

5. At cone 4, the player finishes the choreography by taking a shot at the basket.

6. The player completes the drill five times on each side of the basket.

Coaching Point

To keep space from the defense, the player must stop the outside pivot when the inside shoulder points to the basket. Continuing the pivot until each shoulder is squared to the basket will eliminate the space that was just gained from the defender, thus negating an attempt at a high-percentage shot.

European Step

The European step, or Euro-step, is an offensive footwork maneuver that has gained popularity in the United States in the last decade due to an influx of European players in the NBA. When it is was first introduced, many players were whistled for traveling violations because officials were unfamiliar with this new finishing footwork. Instead of finishing with two forward steps to the basket,

Figure 3.14   Outside pivot game-ready drill.

the Euro-step uses a forward step followed by a lateral step to create space from the defense to open a scoring window.

The Euro-step is most commonly used when an offensive player drives to the basket and a teammate's defender closes out toward the offensive player or tries to take a charge. In either of these scenarios, use the Euro-step. The Euro-step is a two-step move. Pick up the basketball after the last dribble and take a forward step toward the defender to engage them; then, laterally step to the side to create separation for the layup. When you land on the lateral step, lift off the ground and finish with an inside-hand layup (see figure 3.15). The lateral step in the Euro-step will create space and open a scoring window. Ball protection is of utmost importance on a Euro-step due to the closeness of the defense on the first step. Keep the basketball tight to the body in a running-back position with both arms wrapped around the ball, or use your body as a shield between the defender and the ball.

Figure 3.15 Euro-step.

EURO-STEP CHOREOGRAPHY DRILL

Breakdown

Setup

- Use one player and one basketball.
- The player stands at half-court with the ball.

Execution

1. The player gets into a low and athletic stance by bending down and touching the basketball to the ground.

2. The player takes two steps without a dribble. The first step (right foot forward) is short and the second step (left foot lateral) is long.

3. The player then explodes off the ground and shoots a right-hand (inside hand) layup straight up in the air (figure 3.16).

4. The player then catches the ball and returns to a low and athletic stance by bending down and touching the basketball to the ground.

5. The player continues by taking two steps without a dribble. The first step is short (left foot forward) and the second step is long (right foot lateral).

6. The player then explodes off the ground and shoots a left-hand (inside hand) layup straight up in air.

7. The player repeats these steps and stops at the opposite baseline.

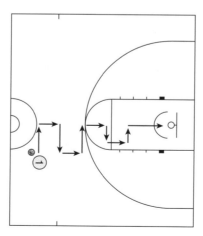

Figure 3.16   Euro-step choreography drill.

EURO-STEP CONE DRILL PART 1

Breakdown

Setup

- Use one player, one basketball, and three cones.
- The player has the ball and faces cone 1.

Execution

1. The player gets into a low and athletic stance by bending down and touching the basketball to the ground.

2. The player then takes two steps without a dribble. The first step is short (right-foot forward toward cone 1) and the second step is long (left-foot lateral outside cone 2).

3. The player then explodes off the ground and shoots a right-hand (inside hand) layup (figure 3.17).

4. The player returns to the start position in front of cone 1 and repeats the drill by taking two steps without a dribble. The first step is short (left-foot forward) and the second step is long (right-foot lateral outside cone 3).

5. The player then explodes off the ground and shoots a left-hand (inside hand) layup.

6. The player completes five Euro-step layups from each side.

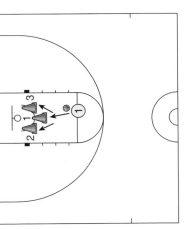

Figure 3.17 Euro-step cone drill part 1.

EURO-STEP CONE DRILL PART 2

Setup

- Use three cones, one player, and one basketball.

Execution

1. Player 1 starts with a basketball in the lane under the rim.

2. Player 1 begins by dribbling outside and around cone 2 and attacking toward cone 1.

3. Player 1 picks up the dribble in front of cone 1 and executes a Euro-step finish at the rim.

4. Player 1 continues by dribbling outside and around cone 3 and attacking toward cone 1 (figure 3.18).

5. Player 1 picks up the dribble in front of cone 1 and executes a Euro-step layup with the opposite footwork and hand.

6. Complete 5 Euro-step layups on each side of the basket.

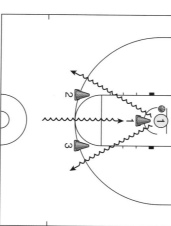

Figure 3.18 Euro-step cone drill part 2.

Floater

The floater is a great equalizer for a smaller player. It is used to finish over bigger help defenders near the basket. The floater is a high-arching shot; the player lifts the shot well above the reach of the defender's outstretched arms and then it moves straight through the bottom of the net. A proficient floater can be a very challenging inside shot to defend.

When you are attacking the basket and the help defender retreats to protect the rim, shoot a floater. Pick up the ball and take two forward steps. The first step is long and the second step is short. Continue by jumping high off the ground on one foot and shooting a floater. If you jump off the right foot, shoot the floater with the left hand. If you jump off the left foot, shoot the floater with the right hand. The apex of the shot should reach the height of the top of the backboard to beat the defender's reach (see figure 3.19). The jump is high, but there is no forward momentum. Jump and land in the same spot to avoid committing a charging foul.

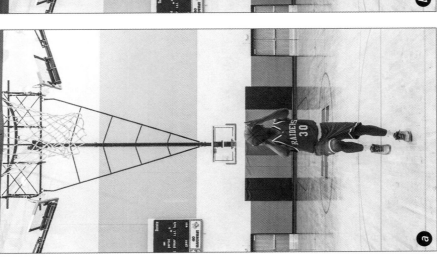

Figure 3.19   Floater.

FLOATER CHOREOGRAPHY DRILL

Breakdown

Setup

- Use one player and one basketball.
- The player stands on the baseline with the ball.

Execution

1. The player gets into a low and athletic stance by bending down and touching the basketball to the ground.

2. The player takes two steps forward without a dribble. The first step (with the right foot) is long and the second step (with the left foot) is short.

3. The player then explodes off the ground and shoots a right-hand floater straight up in the air and returns to the ground in the same spot (figure 3.20).

4. The apex of the shot should reach the height of the top of the backboard.

5. The player then catches the ball and returns to a low and athletic stance by bending down and touching the basketball to the ground.

6. The player again takes two steps without a dribble. The first step (with the left foot) is long and the second step (with the right foot) is short.

7. The player then explodes off the ground and shoots a left-hand floater straight up in air and returns to the ground in the same spot.

8. The apex of the shot should reach the height of the top of the backboard.

9. The player repeats these steps in a straight-line motion and stops on the opposite baseline.

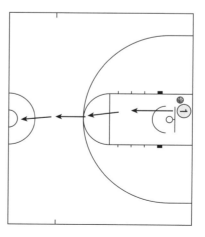

Figure 3.20 Floater choreography drill.

FLOATER CONE DRILL

Breakdown

Setup

- Use one player, one basketball, and five cones.
- The player starts with the ball at half-court.

Execution

1. The player gets into a low and athletic stance by bending down and touching the basketball to the floor.

2. The player takes two steps forward toward the cone. The first step (right foot) is long and the second step (left foot) is short.

3. The player then jumps high and shoots a right-hand floater straight up in the air and returns to the ground in the same spot (figure 3.21).

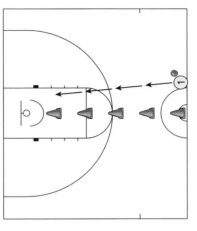

Figure 3.21   Floater cone drill.

4. The apex of the shot should reach the height of the top of the backboard.

5. The player then repeats the drill at each of the remaining cones.

6. At the last cone, the player shoots the floater at the basket.

7. The player repeats the drill with the left hand and the opposite footwork.

8. The player completes five repetitions with each hand.

GAME-READY FLOATER DRILL

Breakdown

Setup

- Use one player, one ball, and two cones.
- The player stands under the rim with the ball.

Execution

1. The player dribbles around cone 1 at the top of the key.

2. The player then attacks toward cone 2 in the lane.

3. At cone 2, the player shoots a floater (figure 3.22).

4. The player completes five floaters with each hand.

Coaching Point

To ensure that the player is jumping up and not out, stick a piece of tape to the inside of the lane. Instruct the player to jump and land on the tape. This simple teaching point will help prevent an errant charging violation during game play.

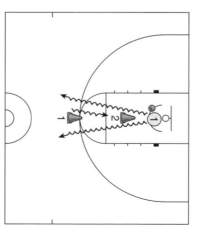

Figure 3.22 Game-ready floater drill.

REFINEMENT DRILLS

You have now learned the proper fundamentals to finish at and around the rim, and you have also learned several maneuvers that can be used to gain separation. It's time to advance to next section of refinement drills, where you will put your skills to the test in one-on-one drills. This is where the real training begins!

INSIDE-FOOT LAYUP ONE-ON-ONE DRILL

Refinement

Setup

- Use two players, one basketball, and two cones.
- Player 1 starts on the elbow with a basketball; player 2 (on defense) starts on the corresponding low block.

Execution

1. Player 1 must dribble inside and around cone 1; then the player attacks the basket for an inside-foot layup.

2. Player 2 must sprint under and around cone 2 to recover and defend (figure 3.23).

3. One point is awarded for each made basket. Players alternate possession and play to 5 points; then they switch to the opposite side of the basket and repeat.

Coaching Point

The offensive player should use the body as a shield by keeping the basketball on the outside of the body and away from the defender.

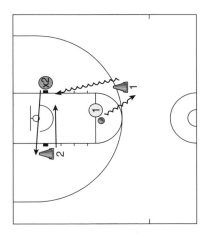

Figure 3.23 Inside-foot layup one-on-one drill.

PIVOT ONE-ON-ONE DRILL

Refinement

Setup

- Use two players and one basketball.
- Players start at the elbow with player 2 (the defender) on the inside.

Execution

1. Player 1 makes the first move; then player 2 can go. Player 1 cannot fake.

2. Player 1 attacks the basket with an outside-hand dribble while player 2 recovers to defend. If player 2 cuts off player 1's path to the basket, player 1 reads and reacts and changes direction with an inside-foot pivot to finish.

3. If player 2 attempts to overextend and block the shot, player 1 reads and reacts and executes an outside pivot finish (figure 3.24).

4. One point is awarded for each made basket. Players alternate possessions and play to 5 points.

5. Players use the left and right sides of the basket.

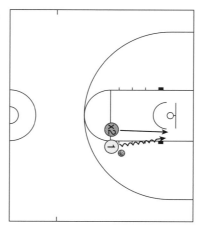

Figure 3.24 Pivot one-on-one drill.

Coaching Point

To reinforce great reads and reactions, award an additional point to the offensive player for each correct pivot.

EURO-STEP ONE-ON-ONE DRILL

Refinement

Setup

- Use two players, one basketball, and two cones.
- Player 1 starts with a basketball on the elbow facing away from the basket.
- Player 2 starts in an athletic stance inside the low block facing away from the basket.

Execution

1. Player 1 initiates the game by dribbling inside and around cone 2 and then attacking the rim for a Euro-step finish.

2. Player 2 responds by sprinting inside and around cone 1 and recovering to defend (figure 3.25).

3. One point is awarded for each made basket. Players alternate possession and play to 5 points; then they repeat the drill on the opposite side of the basket.

Figure 3.25 Euro-step one-on-one drill.

Coaching Point

The Euro-step is most useful when the defender is moving toward the offensive player. The offensive player then uses the Euro-step, changes direction, and attacks the momentum of the defender.

FLOATER ONE-ON-ONE DRILL

Setup

- Use two players, one basketball, and two cones.
- Players start back to back in the middle of the cones, which are on the baseline and the top of the key.

Execution

1. Player 1 initiates the game by dribbling toward and touching cone 2 and attacking toward the rim with a floater finish.

2. Player 2 responds by sprinting and touching cone 1 and recovering to defend player 1 (figure 3.26).

3. One point is awarded for each made basket. Players alternate possession and play to 5 points.

Coaching Point

The floater is most useful when the defender attempts to protect the rim and prevent a layup or dunk. The offensive player takes advantage of this by shooting the floater before arriving at the rim.

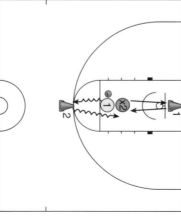

Figure 3.26   Floater one-on-one drill.

FULL-COURT FINISHING ONE-ON-ONE DRILL

Refinement

Setup

- Use two players, one basketball, and four cones.
- Players start on each block facing up the court and away from the basket. Player 1 has the ball.

Execution

1. Player 1 makes the first move; then player 2 can go.

2. Player 1 dribbles the basketball outside and around cone 2 and then dribbles outside and around cone 3.

3. Player 1 then attacks the basket for a layup.

4. While this is happening, player 2 must sprint outside and around cone 1 and outside and around cone 4.

5. Player 2 then sprints diagonally to contest player 1's layup attempt.

6. Players complete the drill on each side of the basket by starting the drill with the basketball on the opposite block (figure 3.27).

7. Players alternate possessions and compete until one player has scored 5 layups.

8. There are to be no shots outside of the lane.

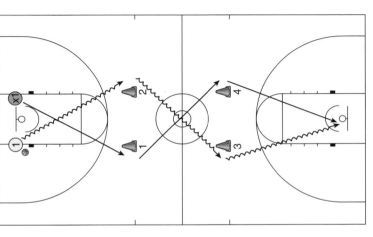

Figure 3.27 Full-court finishing one-on-one drill.

Coaching Point

To ensure the safety of all players involved in this drill, encourage the defender to go for the basketball without making contact with the offensive player's body.

The inside shot is the most commonly taken shot in basketball, but experience has shown me that it is the least practiced. Many players feel they have progressed beyond this shot, and thus they neglect to refine and master it. The inside shot should be more than a shot that you *can* make; it is a shot you *must* make. This level of skill can be developed only through daily repetitions. For example, in 2011, I directed the Stephen Curry Skills Academy. At the academy, Stephen and I trained nearly 30 elite high school and collegiate players. Stephen introduced several drills at the academy that he does in his own personal workouts. One of the drills was an inside shot finishing drill that he does every day. That's right, Stephen Curry, the 2015 NBA MVP, works on inside shots at every practice. That should be a testimony to players and coaches everywhere. Take it from Steph and don't neglect it; perfect it!

Chapter 4

Outside Shots

In the fall of 2012, I conducted a basketball clinic in Virginia for youth players. I had completed my first two sessions with 8- through 17-year-olds, and I had been in the gym for over six hours. I was tired and ready to go home, but I had one more session left with 5- to 7-year-olds. I began the workout by focusing on shot mechanics and form; shortly after that, the players began to take form shots. This was a typical day in the gym, but then *it happened*. I witnessed a moment of accomplishment and pure joy! One young player made the first shot he had ever made in his life. I could tell that it was his first made shot because of his reaction. He celebrated by taking two victory laps around the gym, giving his parents a hug, and giving me a high five. It was a truly special moment for me as a coach, and I will never forget it.

I don't know of any basketball player that doesn't love to shoot and then see and hear the basketball go through the net. Do you remember your first shot? Do you remember the first time you scored in a game? I know that I do. Shooting the basketball is a fun but challenging skill to master, and outside shots are especially difficult. A good outside or perimeter shooter will create a matchup problem for any defense. To defend a good outside shooter, the defender must always remain close to properly contest the shot. This closeness gives the shooter a driving advantage and leaves the defender vulnerable because they have less time and space to react to a drive. A great outside shooting team easily creates more driving, cutting, and post-up opportunities in the lane because each defender is drawn farther away from the basket to defend. Simply put, strong outside shooting makes the defense weak. So, how do you become a great outside shooter? How do you teach players to improve their outside shooting? I created a shooting formula that has been successful with thousands of players: perfect mechanics + game-speed repetitions + game pressure = game shooting success. This chapter will break down the proper mechanics of shooting and outline how to train for the outside shot.

SIX STEPS TO PERFECT MECHANICS

My formula for outside shooting success begins with perfect mechanics. To become a consistent shooter, you must be consistent in your shooting form and mechanics. This form must become a habit, and you must develop muscle memory through daily reinforcement. I heard a great analogy once: Building a consistent shot is a lot like servicing your car. If you want your car to run properly, perform regular maintenance on it. The same is true for your shot. To be a great shooter, do frequent breakdown form shooting drills. In this chapter, I discuss proper form and outline useful drills you can use to learn or correct flaws in your shooting mechanics.

1. Prepared Stance

Let's begin with your stance before you receive the basketball. Begin in a prepared stance with your knees bent, your feet shoulder-width apart, and your weight on the balls of your feet. Your arms are in an L shape with the elbows tucked in at each side, the palms pointing out, and the fingers pointing to the ceiling. If you are a right-handed shooter, your right foot is behind your left; if you are a left-handed shooter, your left foot is behind your right (see figure 4.1). When you catch the ball, square your feet by stepping toward the basketball with the back foot while keeping your front foot planted. When squared, your shooting foot (right foot for right-handed players and left foot for left-handed players) is slightly in front of the planted foot. Catch the basketball high on your shooting side to save time and movement (see figures 4.2 and 4.3). The prepared stance will help you have a quicker release because your body is ready for the shot.

Figure 4.1   Prepared stance before catch.

Figure 4.2   Prepared stance after catch.

Figure 4.3   Feet squared.

2. Hand Placement

The ability to control the basketball is important for every shooter. To ensure ball control, keep the ball on your finger pads and fingertips. Any time the basketball comes in contact with your palm you lose the element of control. You should be able to fit two fingers between the basketball and your palm (see figure 4.4). In addition, spread your fingers as wide as possible to cover more area on the ball (see figure 4.5). Hand placement on the basketball is also vital. Your shooting hand is be below the basketball with your index finger directly in the middle of the ball. The offhand is on the side of the basketball for ball control and to guide the shot. The thumbs form the letter T (see figure 4.6).

Figure 4.4 Basketball out of palm.

Figure 4.5 Fingers spread.

Figure 4.6 Thumbs forming a T.

3. Eyes on the Basket

You can increase your shooting accuracy by having a laser focus. When the ball is in flight, keep your eyes locked on the basket and not on the ball. It is also important to have an open shooting window so your vision is never blocked (see figures 4.7 and 4.8). Place the basketball on your shooting side and not the middle of your body to maintain an open shooting window.

4. Body Control

To ensure a straight-line shot, keep your body squared toward the basket from the beginning of the shot until the end. All 10 toes, your hips, and your shoulders point to the rim (see figure 4.9). Distribute your body weight evenly on the balls of your feet. Without body control, your shot will not stay straight or have the correct trajectory. If your body turns to the left, your shot will miss left. If your body moves forward, your shot will miss long. If your body fades

Figure 4.7   Closed shooting window.

backward, your shot will miss short. Maintain body control and jump and land in the same place with your feet, shoulders, and hips pointing toward the basket. It is also key to release the basketball all in one motion with your knees and your elbows coming to full extension at the same time.

5. Lift Your Shot

Your shot should lift off like a rocket and not like an airplane. Keep your elbow under the basketball to increase the lift of your shot (see figure 4.10). If your shot lifts up like an airplane and your follow-through is in front of your body, the shot will not have adequate arc. A shooter's percentage greatly improves when the basketball lifts off with a high release point. A good way to hold yourself accountable is to release the shot with your shooting elbow at eye level.

Figure 4.8   Open shooting window.

Figure 4.9   Player with hips, shoulders, and toes squared to the rim.

Figure 4.10 Elbow below the basketball and not out.

Figure 4.11 Wrinkle in the wrist.

Let's also talk about your shooting wrist. The wrist is responsible for the backspin on your shot. When loading your shot with your elbow below the ball, check to see if you have a wrinkle in your wrist (figure 4.11). The wrinkle means that your wrist is loaded and ready to fire your shot with backspin. You can't be a consistent shooter without backspin.

6. Follow-Through

Complete your shot by extending your elbows and finishing with a strong and exaggerated flick of the wrist with your shooting hand. The fingers on the shooting hand point toward the ground, and the fingers of the non-shooting hand point upward. The palm of the nonshooting hand faces toward the shooting hand and not toward the basket (see figure 4.12). If the non-shooting hand releases with the palm facing the basket, sidespin will occur and the shot will miss left or right.

Figure 4.12 Perfect follow through.

Checklist for Shooting

1. Prepared stance

- Knees are bent, feet are shoulder-width apart, weight is distributed evenly on the balls of the feet.
- Arms are in the shape of an L, elbows are tucked in at the sides.
- Wrist has a wrinkle, palms are facing the passer.
- Shooting foot is back.
- Feet are squared on catch, shooting foot is slightly in front of pivot foot.

2. Hand placement

- No part of the palm is touching the basketball.
- Index finger of shooting hand is in the middle of the ball.
- Fingers are spread wide.
- Thumbs form a T.

3. Eyes on the basket

- Eyes are locked on the basket and not on the basketball.
- Shooting window is open.

4. Body control

- Feet, shoulders, and hips are pointing toward the basket from the beginning of the shot until the end.
- Shot is one fluid motion, elbows and knees extend at the same time.
- Takeoff and landing are in the same spot or just slightly forward.

5. Lift your shot

- Elbow is under the basketball and not out.
- Wrist has a wrinkle.
- Shooting elbow is at eye level on release.

6. Follow-through

- Elbow extension is exaggerated.
- Elbow is at eye level on release.
- Shooting hand finishes with fingers pointing down.
- Off hand finishes with fingers pointing to the sky and palm facing the shooting hand.

BACKSPIN FORM DRILL

Breakdown

Setup

- Use one player and one basketball.
- The player starts with a basketball but without a basket.

Execution

1. The player starts with the elbow under the basketball and a wrinkle in the wrist; then the player shoots the basketball straight up in the air and exaggerates the release and the wrist flick.

2. The height or apex of the shot should be the same as if the player was shooting at the basket. The player should aim for a point on the floor a few feet in front of them.

3. If proper backspin has been applied, the basketball will repel back toward the player.

4. The player repeats the drill 15 times.

Coaching Point

To increase the challenge, the player can exaggerate the backspin to generate enough spin that the basketball repels over the player's head.

STRAIGHT-LINE SHOOTING DRILL

Breakdown

Setup

- Use one player and one basketball.
- The player starts with the basketball on the half-court line; the player's feet, shoulders, and hips are squared to the line.

Execution

1. The player aims at a point on the half-court line that is about 10 to 12 feet (3-3.5 m) away and takes a shot.

2. The apex or height of the shot should be the same as if the player was shooting at the basket.

3. If the ball hits the half-court line when it descends to the ground, the player is awarded 1 point for an on-target straight-line shot.

4. The player repeats the drill until 10 points are earned.

Coaching Point

Make sure the elbow is under the basketball and that the ball is resting on the finger pads and tips, not the palm of the hand, in order to ensure a straight-line shot.

TIM DUNCAN DRILL

Breakdown

Setup

- Use one player and one basketball.
- Player 1 lies down in a supine position with a basketball.

Execution

1. The player's shooting elbow is tucked tight at the side and underneath the basketball.

2. The player maintains good ball control by keeping the basketball out of the palm and on the finger pads and fingertips. The fingers are spread (figure 4.13a).

3. The player shoots the basketball straight up in the air with one hand and an exaggerated elbow extension and flick of the wrist and holds the follow-through until the basketball returns to the hands (figure 4.13b).

4. If the player has good ball control, the basketball should descend straight back into the hand; if not, the basketball will descend elsewhere.

5. The player repeats the drill 25 times with perfect ball control.

Coaching Point

For ball control, the player should keep the basketball out of the palm and tuck the elbow directly under the basketball.

Figure 4.13 Tim Duncan drill.

Breakdown

nd one basketball.

1 foot (0.3 m) in front of the rim with the ball.

Execution

The purpose of this drill is to remind the player to lift the shot and not push it. The trajectory of a lifted shot gives the player a higher percentage of completion.

1. The player takes a form shot. If the player makes the shot without hitting the rim, the player takes one step back.

2. If the player misses the shot or hits any part of the rim, they must remain in the same spot until they convert an all-net make.

3. The player continues the drill by taking a step back after every all-net make until they reach the three-point line.

Coaching Point

For mastery, have the player attempt five all-net makes in a row.

OFF-HAND FIST DRILL

Breakdown

Setup

- Use one player and one basketball.
- The player starts 1 foot (0.3 m) in front of the rim with the basketball.

Execution

1. The player positions the basketball in the shooting hand with the elbow tucked in at the side directly below the basketball.

2. The player then makes a fist with the offhand and places it on the side of the ball (figure 4.14).

3. The purpose of the fist is to prevent the player's nonshooting hand from influencing the shot and to remind the player that proper shooting form requires a one-hand release.

4. If the player makes the shot, they can take a step back.

5. If the player misses, they continue shooting until the shot is converted.

6. The player repeats the drill by taking a step back after each made shot until the player reaches the three-point line.

Figure 4.14   Off-hand fist drill.

Coaching Point

This is a great drill for a player who uses the offhand in the shot. This drill will help build correct repetition with the guide hand.

FROZEN FREE THROWS DRILL

Breakdown

Setup

- Use one player and one basketball.
- The player starts with the basketball at the free-throw line.

Execution

1. The player shoots the basketball, exaggerates the full elbow extension and flick of the wrist, and holds the follow-through high and extended.
2. The player must hold this follow-through until the basketball hits the ground. This exaggeration will help to reinforce the follow-through.
3. The player repeats the drill until 10 shots are made.

Coaching Point

When teaching a player about the release point on their follow-through, I encourage them to self-correct as they shoot. If they miss short, the player should lower their release point gradually to increase the distance on their next shot. If they miss long, the player should raise their release point gradually to decrease the distance on the next shot.

PREPARED STANCE DRILL

Breakdown

Setup

- Use two players, one basketball, and one cone.
- Player 1 starts at the free-throw line next to the cone; player 2 begins under the rim with the basketball.

Execution

1. Player 1 gets into a prepared stance by bending low and touching the cone. (The cone holds player 1 accountable for starting in a prepared stance.)
2. When player 1 is in a prepared stance, player 2 makes a pass to player 1; then, player 1 squares the feet and shoots.
3. Players repeat the drill until player 1 has made 10 shots and then switch positions.

Coaching Point

The player's entire body should be prepared for the shot before the catch: elbows in, wrinkles in the wrist, and body squared to the target.

KEVIN EASTMAN SQUARE-UP DRILL

Breakdown

Setup

- Use two players and one basketball.

- Player 2 starts with the basketball at the free throw-line and faces the basket; player 1 starts under the basket and faces player 1.

Execution

The purpose of the drill is to help players square their bodies with control and balance in a game-related scenario.

1. Player 2 tosses the basketball in a random direction within the three-point arc.

2. Player 1 must then sprint to the basketball, catch it on the first bounce, and square to the rim for the shot (figure 4.15).

3. Players repeat the drill until they have each made 10 shots.

Coaching Point

This is a great progression drill that helps with body control with shots on the move. To help with deceleration on the catch, remind players to sink slightly into the stance as they retrieve the basketball.

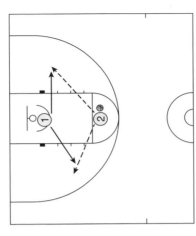

Figure 4.15 Kevin Eastman square-up drill.

MID-RANGE AND LONG-RANGE SHOTS

Outside shots can be categorized into mid-range and long-range shots. The mid-range shot is any shot from 11 feet (3.4 m) to just inside the three-point arc. The long-range shot is any shot at or beyond the three-point arc. Since the addition of the three-point shot in the 1980s, critics say the mid-range shot is a lost art because many players neglect to practice this closer, less-exciting, two-point shot. If you are going to be a great shooter, you can't have weaknesses in your shooting arsenal. You must be able make mid-range and long-range shots and be able to shoot them in any of the game scenarios. There are many ways players come into their shots; they might shoot off a cut, on the move, or off the dribble, just to name a few. In the refinement drills later in the chapter, you will work on the mid-range and long-range shots and learn numerous ways that you can come into your shots.

GAME SPEED

The second ingredient to our outside shooting formula is practicing at a speed that is equal to or greater than game speed. As I mentioned previously, I have been blessed to spend time with Stephen Curry at his 2011 skills academy. He is the best shooter in the NBA today, and he is arguably the greatest shooter ever. His ability to shoot accurately while being closely guarded or while going full speed off the dribble or off a cut is unmatched. He takes and routinely makes tough shots. In my time with him, I asked an important question: "Steph, how do I teach younger players to shoot the basketball like you do?" He replied, "Players don't understand how hard I go in my shooting drills and how fast I go. Everything is faster than game speed." It is important to train at a speed that is faster than game speed. To a great shooter, fast is never fast enough when practicing shooting.

GAME PRESSURE

The last component to our outside shooting formula is practicing with game pressure. I once heard a story about hall of famer Pete Maravich. When he was young, his dad would make him shoot free throws before he went to bed. Pete wouldn't just shoot 100 free throws or make 100 free throws; he would make 100 free throws in a row. That's a very challenging task for any level of basketball player, let alone a child. Pete felt pressure on each and every shot. It didn't matter if the missed shot 1 or shot 91; he had to start over. This an example of practicing with game pressure. You don't have to make 100 shots in a row like Pete did, but have high standards for your shooting in practice. If you expect more in practice, you will achieve more in games. It is important that you learn from great shooters, like Pete, who attached game pressure to his practice shots. If you don't have gamelike pressure in practice, you will not be prepared for the game shots.

FREE THROWS

The free throw is an uncontended shot that is awarded when a player is fouled in the act of shooting, when a foul occurs and the player's team is in the bonus, or when a flagrant or technical foul is committed. A good free-throw shooter should be able to convert on at least 80 percent of their free-throw attempts. Improving your free-throw shooting requires perfect form and numerous repetitions with game-simulated pressure.

When you first come to the free-throw line, get in line with the basket by placing your shooting foot directly on the nail. The nail is found on every court in the center of the free-throw line; it is aligned with the front of the rim. If you take the time to align your shooting foot with the nail, you will be perfectly aligned with the rim. Next, formulate a free-throw routine that you will perform each time you take your shot. For example, many players take multiple dribbles, spin the ball, and take a deep breath. Find a routine that makes you feel more confident and comfortable and use it before every free-throw attempt. When shooting a free throw, do not cross or touch the free-throw line with your feet; this is a violation that results in a forfeit of that attempt. Avoid this by staying on the ground during the shot. Generate power for the shot by bending the knees slightly, and release the shot by extending your elbows and knees simultaneously and raising up high on your toes. The release of the free throw shares many of the same shooting mechanics you learned previously. Review the shooting checklist earlier in the chapter and make sure your mechanics are perfect.

REFINEMENT DRILLS

You have now learned the proper fundamentals of outside shooting. It's time to advance to next section of refinement drills, where you will put your skills to the test. This is where the real training begins!

ONE-MINUTE MID-RANGE DRILL

Refinement

Setup

- Use one player and one basketball.
- The player starts with the basketball under the rim.

Execution

1. The player flips the basketball onto the court, catches it on the first bounce, and takes a mid-range shot.
2. The player rebounds the ball and repeats step 1.
3. The player continues the drill for one minute. All shots should be taken from 12 to 15 feet (3.7-4.6 m).
4. The player records 1 point for every made shot.

Coaching Point

Players should train at a speed that is faster than game speed.

Scorecard

Junior varsity: 3 to 5 points

Varsity: 6 to 8 points

All-conference: 9 to 11 points

All-American: 12 or more points

ONE-MINUTE THREE-POINTERS DRILL

Refinement

Setup

- Use one player and one basketball.
- The player starts with the basketball under the rim.

Execution

1. The player flips the basketball onto the court beyond the three-point line, catches it on the first bounce, and squares to the rim to take a three-point shot.

2. The player rebounds the ball and repeats step 1.

3. The player continues the drill for one minute.

4. The player records 1 point for every made shot.

Coaching Point

To maximize scoring potential, the player should attempt to rebound each shot before the basketball hits the floor.

Scorecard

Junior varsity: 1 to 3 points

Varsity: 4 to 6 points

All-conference: 7 to 9 points

All-American: 10 or more points

ELBOW-TO-ELBOW SHOOTING DRILL

Refinement

Setup

- Use two players and one basketball.
- Player 1 begins at the elbow and player 2 starts under the rim with the basketball.

Execution

1. Player 2 passes the ball to player 1 for the elbow shot.
2. Player 1 alternates between taking mid-range shots from the right and left elbows while player 2 rebounds.
3. Player 1 continues the drill for 60 seconds.
4. Player 1 records 1 point for every made shot and then switches positions with player 2.

Coaching Point

To maximize scoring potential, the shooter should move from one elbow to the other while the ball is in the air.

Scorecard

Junior varsity: 7 to 9 points

Varsity: 10 to 12 points

All-conference: 13 to 15 points

All-American: 16 or more points

WING-TO-CORNER SHOOTING DRILL

Refinement

Setup

- Use two players and one basketball.

Execution

1. Player 1 alternates between taking mid-range corner shots and mid-range wing shots while player 2 rebounds and passes.

2. Player 1 continues the drill for 60 seconds and then performs the drill again on the opposite side of the court.

3. Player 1 records 1 point for every made shot.

Coaching Point

The shooter should maintain a low and prepared stance for the duration of the drill.

Scorecard

Junior varsity: 7 to 9 points

Varsity: 10 to 12 points

All-conference: 13 to 15 points

All-American: 16 or more points

MID-RANGE MASTERY DRILL

Refinement

Setup

- Use two players and one basketball.

Execution

1. Player 1 must complete five out of seven listed spots in under two minutes while player 2 rebounds and passes (figure 4.16).

2. If Player 1 is unable to convert on five out of seven shots at a particular spot, the player tries again at the current spot.

3. Player 1 records the score by recording how many spots that five out of seven shots were completed in two minutes.

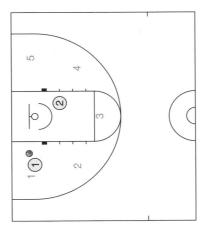

Figure 4.16   Mid-range mastery drill.

Coaching Point

Even though accuracy is the goal, players should maintain a drill speed that is comparable to game speed.

Scorecard

Junior varsity: 1 to 2 spots

Varsity: 3 spots

All-conference: 4 spots

All-American: 5 spots

LONG-RANGE MASTERY DRILL

Refinement

Setup

- Use two players and one basketball.

Execution

1. Player 1 must complete three out of five shots from each of the five listed spots in under two minutes while player 2 rebounds (figure 4.17).

2. If Player 1 is unable to convert on three out of five shots at a particular spot, the player tries again at the current spot.

3. Player 1 records the score by recording how many spots that three out of five shots were completed in two minutes.

Coaching Point

Start low on the catch and use your legs to increase the distance on the long range shot.

Scorecard

Junior varsity: 1 to 2 spots

Varsity: 3 spots

All-conference: 4 spots

All-American: 5 spots

Figure 4.17 Long-range mastery drill.

ONE- AND TWO-DRIBBLE PULL-UP DRILL

Refinement

Setup

- Use two players and one basketball.
- Player 1 is at the top of the key in an athletic stance with the ball; player 2 is under the basket.

Execution

1. Player 1 takes one dribble to the right for a pull-up jump shot and then backpedals to the top of the key while player 2 rebounds and passes back to player 1.

2. Next, player 1 takes two dribbles to the right for a pull-up jump shot and then backpedals to the top of the key while player 2 rebounds and passes back to player 1.

3. Player 1 repeats the drill on the left side with a one-dribble pull-up jump shot followed by a two-dribble pull-up jump shot (figure 4.18).

4. Player 1 continues the drill for two minutes.

5. Player 1 records 1 point for every made shot.

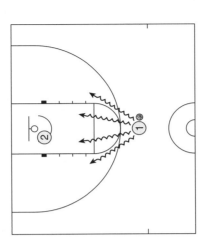

Figure 4.18 One- and two-dribble pull-up drill.

Coaching Point

Pound the dribbles to ensure a quick shot. A fast dribble equates to a fast shot.

Scorecard

Junior varsity: 6 to 10 points

Varsity: 11 to 15 points

All-conference: 16 to 20 points

All-American: 21 points or more.

ACCELERATED GAME SHOTS DRILL

Setup

- Use three players, two basketballs, and five cones.
- Players 2 and 3 each have a basketball.

Execution

1. Player 3 passes to player 2. Player 2 passes to player 1. Player 1 shoots (figure 4.19).

2. If Player 1 misses a shot, one point is awarded.

3. If Player 1 makes the shot but the ball makes contact with the rim, two points are awarded.

4. If Player 1 makes the shot and it goes through the net without touching the rim, three points are awarded.

5. Player 1 shoots for 60 seconds.

6. Player 1 repeats the drill at each of the five listed spots.

Figure 4.19 Accelerated game shots drill.

Coaching Point

This drill accelerates the speed of the shot. The player in the passing position should complete the pass to the shooter as this player is descending from the previous shot.

Scorecard

Junior varsity: 15 to 24 points

Varsity: 25 to 34 points

All-conference: 35 to 44 points

All-American: 45 or more points

BACK-TO-BACK FREE THROWS DRILL

Refinement

Setup

- Use two players and one basketball.
- Player 1 starts with a basketball at the free-throw line; player 2 is under the rim. There are 10 minutes on the clock.

Execution

1. The clock starts after player 1's first free-throw attempt.
2. Player 1 shoots free throws for 10 minutes using the same free-throw routine for each shot while player 2 rebounds.
3. At the end of the 10 minutes, player 1 records their highest number of consecutive free throws made during the drill.

Coaching Point

The player should go through the full free-throw routine and not worry about the clock. The player should focus on mechanics and on keeping the mind clear of doubt.

Scorecard

Junior varsity: 1 to 3 in a row

Varsity: 4 to 6 in a row

All-conference: 7 to 9 in a row

All-American: 10 or more in a row

You now have the drills and tools you need to make your outside shooting better. It's time to get to work and master outside shooting!

Chapter 5

Getting Open

The ability to move without the basketball is important in any type of offensive set or play. Players must be able to get open on their own in one-on-one settings, and they must also be skilled at playing in tandems and setting or using screens to get each other open. Mastering these skills requires sound fundamentals, understanding of proper reads and reactions, and repetition. Did you know that the majority of any basketball player's time on the court is without the ball? It's true! Does that mean a player does not affect the game if the basketball is not in their hands? Does a player's role on the team diminish without the basketball? Absolutely not! The goal of this chapter is for you to learn how to be a player without the basketball.

CUTTING FUNDAMENTALS

Back in 2012, I conducted a basketball clinic in the province of Limburg, Belgium, for youth boys and girls. It was a great learning experience for all the players and coaches involved. I remember one segment in particular in which I began to teach the players how to set and use screens. The director of the camp politely interrupted me, and we had a private conversation. He explained that in their local curriculum they do not teach setting or using screens until the players are much older. He said that it is imperative that players gain a mastery of getting open on their own before screening is introduced. I acknowledged the director and backtracked to teach a full segment of one-on-one cutting maneuvers and techniques. I liked their local progression so much that I adopted it into my personal curriculum after the camp. Proficiency as a cutter takes a lot of repetition, and sometimes coaches don't allow enough time for this to develop. A proficient cutter should have the ability to get open at any time against any defender. By getting open, the player is able to initiate or continue the movements of an offensive set and create their own high-percentage scoring opportunities. Becoming a proficient cutter requires sound fundamentals and proper technical execution. I will first discuss successful habits that all cutters should display. To help you remember these habits, they all begin with the letter S. Second, I will show you how to implement these fundamentals into common offensive maneuvers to get open in the post and the perimeter.

Scoring Spot

When cutting and attempting to get open, where is the best location to receive a pass? Always seek to receive a pass in a scoring spot. A scoring spot is an area on the court from which you can effectively shoot and score. Too often, I see players at all levels cut and receive passes 30 feet from the basket where they are ineffective. Make it a priority to receive the basketball where you want to receive it and not where the defender wants you to.

Stance

As you have learned in previous chapters, the athletic stance gives you an advantage. Keep the knees slightly bent, the feet shoulder-width apart, the back straight, and your weight slightly forward. Playing without the basketball is a footrace that requires sudden changes of direction and speed and the ability to absorb physical contact. Maintain a low and athletic stance to keep balance and body control and to maximize athleticism.

Setup

Set up the cut by using a deceptive fake to get open. If you want to get open high, set up your cut by faking low. If you want to get open on the right, set up your cut by faking left. The key to a good fake is to sell it with the entire body. If you don't sell it, the defense won't buy it. Sell it with a short and violent foot fake while shifting your weight and your eyes in the direction of the fake. Make sure that the fake is short and not long so as to ensure body control and balance. Short fakes get the defense off balance, while long fakes will get you off balance. Setting up the cut with a quality fake will give you an early advantage on your defender.

Sprint

When the advantage is gained by a deceptive fake, finish the cut with a sprint. Watch any great player off the ball and you will see them pursue the basketball by sprinting after the fake with great urgency. The early advantage that a quality fake gains you is of no value if you don't follow it up by sprinting to your desired location.

Show Hands

Give the passer a target by showing outstretched hands with all 10 fingers pointed toward the ceiling. Showing your hands is a nonverbal way to let the ball handler know that you are open, and it also gets you prepared to catch and receive the basketball.

See the Ball

A golden rule of moving without the basketball is to always know where the basketball is on the floor. It's difficult to make the correct cut if you're not aware of where the basketball is or what the ball handler is doing. Seeing the basketball also limits turnovers because you are constantly available and ready to receive a pass if needed.

Speak

If you want it, say so! If you are open, demand the basketball by calling the ball handler's name with a strong tone and communicating your location on the court (e.g., "Marcus! Ball! On your right! In the corner!").

Cut Slow and Then Go

The offensive player is in control because they know when they are going to start, stop, or change direction; all the defender can do is try to anticipate the next move. I've observed many players who were exceptionally fast but still had a tough time creating separation from their defenders. Why? Because they *constantly* moved fast. I teach players to change their speed by telling them to "cut slow and then go." Playing at the same speed will allow the defender to easily anticipate your moves, but sudden and exaggerated changes of speed will make you tough to read and will create space from the defense.

Spread Out

Spacing is another foundational rule when moving without the basketball. Seek to keep a cushion of 15 to 18 feet (4.6-5.5 m) between you and your nearest teammates. Failure to keep space allows one defender to easily guard two offensive players. You can never go wrong by creating more space on the floor for yourself and your teammates.

ONE-ON-ONE PERIMETER MOVES

The ability to get open without the basketball in the one-on-one setting is an important part of any type of offense. Next, I will review a few basic maneuvers for gaining space and separation against any defender.

V-Cut

The V-cut is the most common maneuver to get open without the basketball. The V-cut is a low to high cut that helps you gain separation and space on the perimeter. It is termed a V-cut because the path of the cut is similar to the shape of the letter V. Execute the cut by starting in a low and athletic stance; then walk with your defender to a lower position on the court. Plant your inside foot, unexpectedly change direction, sprint high, and prepare to receive a pass with your hands outstretched and your eyes on the ball handler. In a loud and confident tone, call the ball handler's name and give your location on the court. Finish the cut by receiving the pass, squaring to the rim, and entering the triple-threat position (see figure 5.1a through c).

Figure 5.1 V-cut.

a

Figure 5.1 *(continued)* V-cut.

TWO-BALL V-CUT DRILL

Breakdown

Setup

- Use two players and two basketballs.
- Player 1 dribbles two balls outside the top of the key; player 2 is at the low block.

Execution

1. While player 1 is dribbling the balls, player 2 executes a V-cut and sprints to the wing.

2. Player 1 reacts to the cut and completes an air pass to player 2 with the outside hand (figure 5.2).

3. Player 2 catches the ball and drives to the basket for a layup.

4. Player 1 then takes two dribbles to the free-throw line and takes a shot with the remaining basketball.

5. Players repeat the drill five times from each side of the court.

Figure 5.2   Two-ball v-cut drill.

Coaching Point

Even though this drill isn't against a defender, each offensive player should play at game speed. This is where great habits are developed. A saying that I commonly repeat at my practices is "whatever you do in practice you will do in the game."

L-Cut

The L-cut allows the cutter to get open more easily against a physical defender. It is termed an L-cut because the path of the cut is similar to the shape of the letter L. Execute the L-cut by starting in a low and athletic stance on the block; then, walk your defender slowly up the lane toward the elbow. When you arrive at the elbow, fight to gain an inside position between the defender and the wing by stepping across the defender's body with your inside foot. Once you have the inside position, sprint to the wing with your hands outstretched and your eyes on the ball handler. In a loud and confident tone, call the ball handler's name and give your location on the court. Finish the cut by receiving the pass, squaring to the rim, and entering the triple-threat position (see figure 5.3).

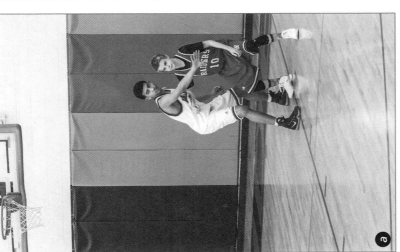

Figure 5.3 L-cut.

TWO-BALL L-CUT DRILL

Breakdown

Setup

- Use two players and two basketballs.
- Player 1 dribbles two balls outside the top of the key; player 2 is at the low block.

Execution

1. While player 1 is dribbling the balls, player 2 executes an L-cut and sprints to the wing.

2. Player 1 reacts to the cut and completes an air pass to player 2 with the outside hand (figure 5.4).

3. Player 2 catches the ball and takes a perimeter shot.

4. Player 1 then takes two dribbles to the free-throw line and takes a shot with the remaining basketball.

5. Players repeat the drill five times from each side of the court.

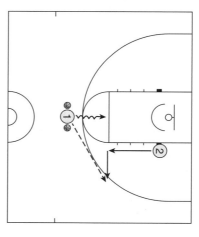

Figure 5.4 Two-ball L-cut drill.

Coaching Point

Players should change their speed on the cut each time they go. They should be unpredictable regarding when they will start, stop, and change direction.

Backdoor Cut

The backdoor cut is the great equalizer against an overly aggressive defender. The back door is a surprise cut toward the rim that should be executed anytime there is not a defender between the cutter and the basket or when the cutter's defender has lost visual contact with them. It is most commonly used at the end of a low-to-high cut on the perimeter, such as a V-cut or an L-cut. If the cutter cuts high and the defender attempts to take away the passing lane by stepping between the cutter and the ball handler, the cutter should use the backdoor cut. To execute the backdoor cut, set it up by remaining in a low and athletic stance and extending your outside hand as if you are ready to receive a pass. One of my mentors once said that you must "yell to sell" a backdoor cut. As you extend the outside hand, yell for the basketball with a sense of urgency. When the defender gets out of position, plant and push off of the outside foot and unexpectedly change direction and sprint toward the basket. The ball handler reacts by making a penetrating bounce or lob pass to you for a high-percentage inside shot (see figure 5.5).

Figure 5.5 Backdoor cut.

TWO-BALL BACKDOOR CUT DRILL

Breakdown

Setup

- Use two players and two basketballs.
- Player 1 dribbles two balls outside the top of the key; player 2 is at the low block.

Execution

1. While player 1 is dribbling the balls, player 2 executes a V-cut and sprints to the wing.

2. At the wing, player 2 extends the outside hand, plants the outside foot, and calls for the basketball.

3. Player 2 then changes direction and cuts toward the basket in a straight line.

4. Player 1 reacts to the cut and completes a bounce pass with the outside hand to player 2 (figure 5.6).

5. Player 2 catches the ball and takes a layup.

6. Player 1 then takes two dribbles to the free-throw line and takes a shot with the remaining basketball.

7. Players repeat the drill five times from each side of the court.

Figure 5.6 Two-ball backdoor-cut drill.

Coaching Point

The instruction I give my players as they change direction on the backdoor cut is "plant-push." I want the plant to be like a jab step instead of a stop. That way, the defense is engaged high and the cutter is able to quickly explode low.

ONE-ON-ONE POST MOVES

The best post players move without the basketball and create high-percentage shots for themselves and their team. They constantly seek the basketball by cutting and following it from one side of the floor to the other in order to gain an advantageous position on their defenders, which allows for an easy penetrating pass and a quality field-goal attempt. This is commonly referred to as a block-to-block cut. Here I present two very effective block-to-block cutting maneuvers.

Fake-and-Go

When cutting from one block to the other in search of a post feed, try using the fake-and-go. To execute the fake-and-go, start on the weak-side block. The weak-side block is the low block on the opposite side of the floor as the basketball. While on the weak side, drop into an athletic stance. From here you have the choice to either fake low and cut above the defender to the opposite block or fake high and cut below the defender to the opposite block. Once the fake is made, sprint to the ball-side block with your hands outstretched, demand the basketball, and communicate to the ball handler your location on the court. Finish by establishing great position on the ball-side block with the defender at your back. Hold this advantageous position until the ball handler delivers a penetrating pass (see figure 5.7).

Figure 5.7 Fake-and-go cut.

TWO-BALL FAKE-AND-GO DRILL

Breakdown

Setup

- Use two players and two basketballs.
- Player 1 dribbles two balls on the wing outside the three-point line; player 2 is at the low block on the opposite side of the rim as the ball.

Execution

1. While player 1 is dribbling the balls, player 2 executes a fake-and-go move and cuts to the ball-side low block.

2. Player 1 reacts to the cut and completes a penetrating pass to player 2 (figure 5.8).

3. Player 2 catches the ball and takes an inside shot.

4. Player 1 then takes a stationary perimeter shot with the remaining basketball.

5. Players repeat the drill five times from each side of the court.

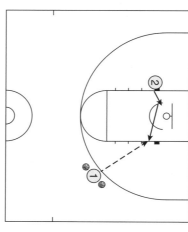

Figure 5.8 Two-ball fake-and-go drill.

Coaching Point

At the end of the cut, make sure the player is positioned above the block so they have the proper angle to score in either direction.

Swim Move

The swim move first originated on the football field. It is used when an offensive player's defender becomes overly aggressive and uses physical contact to prevent a cut from one block to the other. As the cutter, your primary focus when executing the swim move is to remain in a low and athletic stance to maintain balance and body control on the collision. When physical contact occurs and the defender stops your forward movement with a strong arm, first look to parry the strong arm and then attempt to gain the advantage on the defender by swimming your opposite arm over and around the defender's body. If the defender uses their left arm to your chest to block your path, use your right arm to parry and the left arm to swim and gain separation. If the defender uses their right arm to your chest, use your left arm to parry and your right arm to swim over and past the defender to gain separation. Once the swim move has been executed, sprint to the ball-side block with your hands outstretched, demand the basketball, and communicate to the ball handler your location on the court. Finish by establishing great position on the ball-side block with the defender at your back. Hold this advantageous position until the ball handler delivers a penetrating pass (see figure 5.9).

Figure 5.9   Swim move.

TWO-BALL SWIM MOVE DRILL

Breakdown

Setup

- Use two players and two basketballs.
- Player 1 dribbles two balls on the wing outside the three-point line; player 2 is at the low block on the opposite side of rim.

Execution

1. While player 1 is dribbling the balls, player 2 executes a swim move and cuts to the ball-side low block.

2. Player 1 reacts to the cut and completes a penetrating pass to player 2.

3. Player 2 catches the ball and takes an inside shot.

4. Player 1 then takes two dribbles to the elbow and takes a shot with the remaining basketball (figure 5.10).

5. Players repeat the drill five times from each side of the court.

Figure 5.10 Two-ball swim move drill.

Coaching Point

After completing the swim maneuver, the player should cut in a straight line to the opposite block. A straight line is the quickest path between two points.

SCREENING FUNDAMENTALS

Screening is using your body to block the path of a teammate's defender to assist them in gaining separation to get open with or without the basketball. Before I discuss the most common types of screens, let's look at the fundamentals of setting a proper screen.

Set It Up and Then Sprint

Misdirection is important for success with screening. It should be the goal of the screener to arrive at the screen without their defender. This will create a temporary two versus one advantage, which oftentimes leads to early scoring opportunities for both the screener and the cutter. If you want to screen for a teammate with the basketball, first fake away from the ball before sprinting to the ball handler for the screen. If you want to screen for a teammate to the left, first fake to the right before sprinting to set the screen. Always finish by sprinting to set the screen for a teammate. The fake gives you a head start and the sprint ensures that you arrive first.

Split

When sprinting to set a screen, come to a one-brake stop by executing what is commonly referred to as a *jump stop*. Setting screens requires that you absorb a collision or physical contact from the defender whom you are setting a screen on. When you come to this sudden stop, split your feet wide for greater balance and body control and cross your arms in front of your groin for protection. This power stance also makes you a much larger barrier to maneuver around.

Stay

Hold the screen until the cutter or ball handler has exited. The referee will call a foul on you if there is any movement to impede the path of the defender once the screen has been set. You must remain still. The ball handler or cutter can help by waiting on the screen and not going too early. A good rule to follow to avoid this violation is that the screener has control. The ball handler and the cutter cannot move to exit off of the screen until the screener is set and gives them the verbal command "go!"

Back to Attack

The screener's back should point to the area to which they want the cutter to cut. For example, when setting a back screen, angle your screen so your back is pointing to the rim in order to create a better scoring opportunity for the cutter. As a rule, seek to aim your screen for a high-percentage scoring area or for zones on the court that are unoccupied by the defense (see figure 5.11).

Figure 5.11 Proper screening stance.

THE BALL SCREEN

The ball screen occurs when an offensive player sets a screen for the ball handler. The ball screen has become more popular in recent years because it is difficult to defend. The ball screen creates scoring opportunities for the ball handler and the screener, and it also produces mismatches because defenders are sometimes forced to guard an offensive player that is out of their position. The two most common actions off a ball screen are the pick-and-roll and the pick-and-pop. The pick-and-roll occurs when the ball handler attacks off the screen and the screener's defender falls out of position. As the screener, if there is no one between you and the basket, pivot toward the ball handler and cut hard to the rim with outstretched hands while calling for the basketball. The ball handler finishes by executing a penetrating bounce or a lob pass to you for an inside shot (see figure 5.12). The pick-and-pop is a counter to the pick-and-roll and occurs when the

Figure 5.12 Pick-and-roll.

ball handler attacks off the screen and the screener's defender chooses to drift low and below the screen to protect the basket. When this happens, pivot and open up to the ball handler and then quickly backpedal high and away with your hands outstretched while calling for the basketball. The ball handler finishes by completing a pass to you for a mid-range or long-range shot (see figure 5.13).

Figure 5.13 Pick-and-pop.

PICK-AND-ROLL DRILL

Breakdown

Setup

- Use two players and one basketball.
- Player 1 is at the three-point line at the top of the key with the ball; player 2 is at the low block.

Execution

1. Player 2 sprints to player 1 and delivers a ball screen.

2. Player 1 attacks with two dribbles off the screen; player 2 reacts by opening up toward player 1 and rolling to the rim.

3. Player 1 then completes a penetrating pass to player 2 (figure 5.14).

4. Player 2 catches the ball and takes a layup.

5. Players repeat the drill five times from each side of the court.

Coaching Point

The ball handler should set up the ball screen by faking in the opposite direction of the screen.

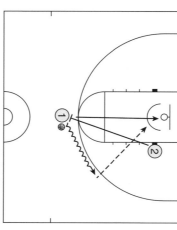

Figure 5.14   Pick-and-roll drill.

PICK-AND-POP DRILL

Breakdown

Setup

- Use two players and one basketball.
- Player 1 is outside the three-point line at the top of the key with the ball; player 2 is at the low block.

Execution

1. Player 2 sprints to player 1 and delivers a ball screen.

2. Player 1 attacks with two dribbles off the screen; player 2 reacts by opening up toward player 1 and backpedaling toward the opposite elbow.

3. Player 1 then completes pass to player 2 (figure 5.15).

4. Player 2 catches the ball and takes a mid-range shot.

5. Players repeat the drill five times from each side of the court.

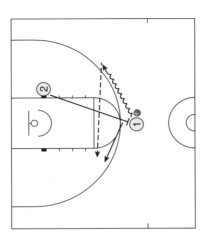

Figure 5.15   Pick-and-pop drill.

Coaching Point

Before receiving the pass, the screener should be in an athletic and prepared stance with hands outstretched. I call this being "shot ready."

THE PIN-DOWN SCREEN

The pin-down screen is most commonly used to help a teammate get open on the wing. It is initiated when an offensive player on the wing sprints to set a screen for a teammate on the low block. The cutter sets up the screen by faking low below the screen with a foot fake with their inside foot (see figure 5.16a). The cutter then cuts tight over the screen by taking their inside shoulder to the screener's hip to ensure that the cutter is the first player over the screen. From this point, the cutter and screener will play as a tandem and read and react to the defense and one another.

Curl

If the cutter's defender trails the cutter over the screen, then the cutter should curl tightly around the screen and toward the basket for an inside shot opportunity. The screener will react to the curl cut by pivoting and opening up toward the ball handler and then backpedaling to the short corner for a second option (see figure 5.16b).

Straight

The straight cut is executed most often when the ball handler is in need of a quick receiver as if to initiate an offense by completing the first pass. The cutter executes the straight cut off the down screen by sprinting in a straight line to the wing for an easy reception. The screener then reacts by pivoting and opening up their body toward the wing in an attempt to gain an advantageous position for an easy penetrating post pass (see figure 5.16c).

Fade

If the cutter's defender cheats and goes under the screen, as if waiting for the offensive player to curl, the cutter should fade. A fade cut is completed by taking one step over the screen as if curling to the rim but then suddenly stopping and changing direction by backpedaling behind and away from the screen for a mid-range shot opportunity. In this situation, the screener would react by first pivoting and opening toward the basketball and then cutting directly to the front of the rim for a second option (see figure 5.16d).

Figure 5.16 Pin-down screen with: (a) start of the action; (b) curl; (c) straight cut; and (d) fade.

TWO-BALL PIN-DOWN DRILL: CURL

Breakdown

Setup

- Use two players and two basketballs.
- Player 1 is on the wing; player 2 is on the low block. The coach is at the top of the key outside the three-point line with two basketballs.

Execution

1. Player 1 sprints to down screen for player 2.

2. Player 2 waits for the screen, executes a curl toward the lane, and receives a pass from the coach for an inside shot.

3. Player 1 reacts to the curl by opening up to the coach and backpedaling to the short corner.

4. The coach then passes a ball to player 1, who takes a stationary mid-range shot (figure 5.17).

5. Players repeat the drill five times on each side of the basket.

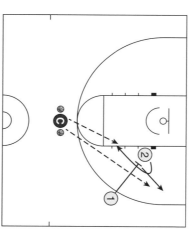

Figure 5.17 Two-ball pin-down drill: curl.

Coaching Point

Be sure to have players work on different levels of the curl cut: high for the elbow shot and low for the inside shot.

TWO-BALL PIN-DOWN DRILL: FADE

Breakdown

Setup

- Use two players and two basketballs.
- Player 1 is on the wing; player 2 is on the low block. The coach is at the top of the key outside the three-point line with two basketballs.

Execution

1. Player 1 sprints to down screen for player 2.

2. Player 2 waits for the screen, executes a fade to the short corner, and receives a pass from the coach for a stationary mid-range shot.

3. Player 1 reacts to the fade by opening up to the coach and cutting to the middle of the rim.

4. The coach then passes the ball to player 1, who takes an inside shot (figure 5.18).

5. Players repeat the drill five times on each side of the basket.

Figure 5.18   Two-ball pin-down drill: fade.

Coaching Point

Player 1 must wait until player 2 exits the screen before executing the cut to the rim. Failure to wait can lead to an offensive foul on the screener.

TWO-BALL PIN-DOWN DRILL: STRAIGHT

Setup

- Use two players and two basketballs.
- Player 1 begins on the wing; player 2 on the low block. The coach is at the top of the key outside the three-point line with two basketballs.

Execution

1. Player 1 sprints to down screen for player 2.

2. Player 2 waits for the screen and then executes a straight cut to the wing and receives a pass from the coach for a stationary perimeter shot.

3. Player 1 reacts to the straight cut by opening up to the coach and cutting to the front of the rim.

4. The coach then throws a penetrating pass to player 1, who takes an inside shot (figure 5.19).

5. Players repeat the drill five times on each side of the basket.

Figure 5.19 Two-ball pin-down drill: straight.

Coaching Point

The straight cut is one of the most common ways that an offensive team gets the basketball to the wing.

BACK SCREEN

The back screen is used to surprise the defense. It is delivered to a defender's back when they are not looking. It is executed when an offensive player occupying a low position on the court, such as the low block, sprints to set a screen for a teammate on the perimeter. The cutter then quickly sets up the screen by faking left or right and then cutting straight to the rim for a high-percentage inside shot. The screener reacts to the cut by lifting high toward the perimeter for a second option (see figure 5.20).

Figure 5.20 Back screen.

TWO-BALL BACK-SCREEN DRILL

Setup

- Use two players and two basketballs.
- Player 1 is on the low block; player 2 is on the wing. The coach stands at the top of key with two basketballs.

Execution

1. Player 1 sprints toward player 2 for a back screen.

2. Player 2 waits for the screen to be set and then executes a cut to the basket.

3. The coach reacts to the cut and delivers a penetrating pass to player 2, who takes a layup; then the coach passes the remaining basketball to player 1, who squares to the rim for a perimeter shot (figure 5.21).

4. Players repeat the drill five times from each side of the floor.

Figure 5.21 Two-ball back-screen drill.

Coaching Point

To sell the screen, the cutter should keep their eyes on the ball handler until the very last moment and then quickly and assertively use the screen for the easy inside shot.

REFINEMENT DRILLS

You now have a firm understanding of the fundamentals of getting open. It's time to advance to the refinement drills where you will compete in one-on-one and three-on-three drills to prepare for game success and mastery. This is where the real training begins!

ONE-ON-ONE PERIMETER DRILL: GETTING OPEN

Refinement

Setup

- Use two players and one basketball.

- Player 1 is on the block on offense; player 2 defends. The coach is at the top of the key outside the three-point line with the basketball.

Execution

1. Player 1 works to get open while player 2 tries for a deflection or a steal; player 1 is confined to one side of the basket and cannot cut to the opposite side (figure 5.22).

2. If player 1 gets open, the coach completes a pass to player 1 and the player receives 1 point and remains on offense.

3. If player 2 creates a deflection or a steal, the possession ends and player 2 is now on offense.

4. Players compete for three minutes. The player with the most points wins.

Figure 5.22 One-on-one perimeter drill: getting open.

Coaching Point

This is a drill that I use at many of my clinics. It's a great drill that results in a tremendous number of correct repetitions.

ONE-ON-ONE POST DRILL: GETTING OPEN

Setup

- Use two players and one basketball.
- Player 1 is on the block on the opposite side of the rim and is on offense; player 2 defends. The coach is on the wing outside the three-point line with the basketball.

Execution

1. Player 1 works to get open by cutting across the lane toward the coach while player 2 tries for a deflection or a steal (figure 5.23).

2. If player 1 gets open, the coach completes a pass to player 1 and the player receives 1 point and remains on offense.

3. If player 2 creates a deflection or a steal, the possession ends and player 2 is now on offense.

4. Each time the drill resets, players must start by occupying the low block opposite the coach.

5. Players compete for three minutes. The player with the most points wins.

Figure 5.23 One-on-one post drill: getting open.

Coaching Point

Getting open in the low post should not be a skill that is limited to post players. We should teach players how to play all positions. Be sure to have your guards working on post skills and your post players working on guard skills.

THREE-ON-THREE BACK-SCREEN DRILL

Refinement

Setup

- Use six players and one basketball.
- Three players are on offense and three are on defense.

Execution

1. Each time a pass is made, one of the offensive players without the ball must immediately set a back screen. Failure to do so will result in a turnover (figure 5.24).

2. The game is live and the offense can score at any time.

3. Each made basket is worth 1 point, and the offensive team retains possession of the basketball after each score.

4. The defense must get a stop to be on offense.

5. The game is played for 10 minutes. The team with the most points wins.

Figure 5.24   Three-on-three back-screen drill.

Coaching Point

Feel free to use your discretion on the rules of the drill. Oftentimes, I will overlook a tandem not setting a back screen after a pass if the pass is made to a player who just used or set a back screen.

THREE-ON-THREE BALL-SCREEN DRILL

Refinement

Setup

- Use six players and one basketball.
- Three players are on offense and three are on defense.

Execution

1. Each time a pass is made, one of the two offensive players without the ball must immediately set a ball screen. Failure to do so will result in a turnover (figure 5.25).

2. The game is live and the offense can score at any time.

3. Each made basket is worth 1 point, and the offensive team retains possession of the basketball after each score.

4. The defense must get a stop to be on offense.

5. The game is played for 10 minutes. The team with the most points wins.

Coaching Point

Feel free to use your discretion on the rules of the drill. Oftentimes, I will overlook a tandem not setting a ball screen after a pass if the pass is made to a player who just used or set a ball screen.

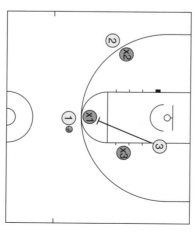

Figure 5.25 Three-on-three ball-screen drill.

THREE-ON-THREE PIN-DOWN DRILL

Refinement

Setup

- Use six players and one basketball.
- Three players are on offense and three are on defense.

Execution

1. Each time a pass is made, one of the offensive players without the ball must immediately set a pin-down screen. Failure to do so will result in a turnover (figure 5.26).

2. The game is live and the offense can score at any time.

3. Each made basket is worth 1 point, and the offensive team retains possession of the basketball after each score.

4. The defense must get a stop to be on offense.

5. The game is played for 10 minutes. The team with the most points wins.

Figure 5.26 Three-on-three pin-down drill.

Coaching Point

Feel free to use your discretion on the rules of the drill. Oftentimes, I will overlook a tandem not setting a pin-down screen after a pass if the pass is made to a player who just used or set a pin-down screen.

To be a productive player in a team setting, you must be able to get open without the basketball and set and use screens. This is a vital part of any team's offense. The next time you watch a collegiate or professional game, study what players do when the basketball is not in their hands. Watch how hard they cut, the ways they set screens and their angles, how they use the screens, and how they read the defense. As mentioned, the vast majority of your time during a basketball game will be without the basketball, and that should be the only motivation you need to dedicate more time in practice to mastering getting yourself and your teammates open.

Chapter 6

Rebounding

Rebounding is a determining factor in the outcome of a game. The team that obtains more rebounds will usually be the victor. Why is that the case? A team can decrease the number of opportunities their opponent has to score by securing a defensive rebound after each attempted shot. A team can also increase their possessions and possibilities to score by pursuing and gaining more offensive rebounds. Simply put, more rebounds mean more opportunities for your team to score and fewer opportunities for the opponent. This is why rebounding is a critical skill to master.

I am beginning to see a worrying trend at basketball practices across all levels: rebounding has become the least-taught and most-overcoached skill in the game today. Coaches don't know how to teach basic rebounding skills, so they provide nebulous instructions to players that aren't helpful. Oftentimes, the only instruction given to a player is "box out" or "get the ball," followed by a lot of shouting. Is that all that is required to be a great rebounder? Are these coaches really giving their players the proper tools to dominate the glass, or are they just coaching effort? Rebounding is a skill, and it needs to be taught from a tactical standpoint. Effort, toughness, and determination are crucial and should be emphasized, but proper technique, dynamic maneuvers, and correct reads and reactions are equally vital to rebounding success. In this chapter, I focus on the technical fundamentals of rebounding, and then I refine those concepts through a series of competitive and intense drills.

DEFENSIVE REBOUNDING TACTICAL FUNDAMENTALS

The fundamental goal of a good defensive rebounding team is to limit the offense to one shot. To achieve this, each defensive player must focus on the following three keys.

Vision and Voice

As a defender, use your peripheral vision to maintain sight of the basketball and your offensive player at all times. For rebounding purposes, seeing both the offensive player and the ball gives you a head start because you can move on the flight of the basketball as it leaves the shooter's hands, and you can keep eye contact with the ball from the beginning of the shot until it hits the rim. You should also use the proper pivot when executing the box out; I will discuss proper pivoting reads in subsequent sections. Once the shot is taken, each defensive player also says the word "shot" so each teammate is prepared for the rebound.

Inside Position

Inside position is the space between your opponent and the basket. As a golden rule, the defensive player always takes the inside position; this prevents the offense from making straight-line cuts to the rim for scoring opportunities, and it gives the defender an advantageous position when a shot is taken. Once the shot goes up, it is harder to maintain this inside position because the offensive player will fight around and through the defender to gain access to the basketball. There are three different techniques that are commonly used to maintain the inside position.

Hit-Go Technique

Use the hit-go technique to stop your opponent's path to the rebound by striking them with a forearm to the chest. As soon as contact is made and the opponent's forward progress is momentarily stopped, break contact and sprint to pursue the basketball. It is important to keep the elbow bent and to generate power from the lower body and not the arm. Exerting power from the upper body by extending the elbow will result in a foul.

HIT-GO DRILL

Breakdown

Setup

- Use one player and one blocking pad.
- This drill is executed without a basketball. The player is inside the lane. The coach has the blocking pad and is outside the three-point arc.

Execution

1. The coach blows the whistle.
2. The player sprints toward the coach with short, choppy steps and blasts the coach with a bent forearm to the chest.
3. The player then immediately sprints toward the rim, leaps off the ground, and secures the imaginary basketball.
4. The player repeats the drill 10 times.

Coaching Point

A player should make contact with their forearm to the opponent's chest for only a moment before releasing contact to pursue the basketball.

Boxout Technique

Use the boxout technique to stop your opponent's path to the basketball by striking them with a bent forearm to the chest, making a front or reverse pivot, and ending with your posterior against the opponent's thighs and your back to the opponent's chest. When boxing out, keep your hands and arms high above your head and in the shape of a field-goal post to prevent your opponent from reaching over you for the basketball. When the basketball hits the rim, break contact with your opponent and pursue the ball.

BOXOUT DRILL

Breakdown

Setup

- Use one player and one blocking pad.

- This drill is executed without a basketball. The player is inside the lane. The coach has the blocking pad and is outside the three-point arc.

Execution

1. The coach blows the whistle.

2. The player sprints toward the coach with short, choppy steps; blasts the coach with a bent forearm to the chest; and makes a front-pivot or reverse-pivot boxout.

3. The player holds the boxout while driving the coach back until the coach blows the whistle again.

4. On the second whistle, the player sprints toward the rim, leaps off of the ground, and secures the imaginary basketball.

5. The player repeats the drill 10 times.

Coaching Point

The player should aggressively pursue the boxout with the goal of not allowing the coach to enter the lane.

Chest-Out Technique

The chest-out technique is an emergency maneuver you can use when your opponent has forced you low and below the rim and thus negated your dominant inside position. In this situation, quickly turn and face your opponent, lift your hands high above your head, get low and wide at the base, and subtly push your opponent out and away from the basket with your hips. This technique may not allow you to secure the rebound, but it will help to prevent your opponent from obtaining it.

CHEST-OUT DRILL
Breakdown

Setup

- Use one player and one blocking pad.
- This drill is executed without a basketball. The player is in the inside position under the rim. The coach has the blocking pad and is inside the paint in front of the rim.

Execution

1. The coach blows the whistle.
2. The player turns toward the coach and executes a chest-out move.
3. The player holds the chest out while driving the coach back until the coach blows the whistle.
4. On the second whistle, the drill stops.
5. The player repeats the drill 10 times.

Coaching Point

Make sure the player's hands are high and above the head to create a barrier for the opponent to rebound through.

Pursuit

Once you've executed one of the previous techniques to maintain inside position, you must immediately pursue the basketball with relentless determination. That means you must sprint and jump high! As a rule, release contact from your opponent once the basketball hits the rim. Time your release so you can retrieve the basketball at the apex of the opponent's jump. Remember to always secure the basketball with two hands and tuck it under your chin for protection. When you return to the ground, enter a low and wide stance to ensure balance and body control.

BACKBOARD CATCH-AND-CHIN DRILL

Breakdown

Setup

- Use one player and one basketball.
- The player has the ball and is in front of the rim facing the backboard.

Execution

1. The player tosses the basketball off the backboard.
2. The player then leaps off of the ground, catches the basketball with two hands at the apex of the jump, and lands with a wide base to ensure body control and balance. The player protects the basketball by securing it under the chin and tight to the body.
3. The player repeats the drill 12 times.
4. On the 12th repetition, the player finishes the drill with a strong, two-hand power layup.

Coaching Point

When obtaining the rebound, make sure to have the elbows out and not in to secure the inside position and space for the shot.

REBOUNDING PURSUIT DRILL

Breakdown

Setup

- Use one player and one basketball.
- The player has the ball and is outside the lane on the right side of the basket.

Execution

1. The player tosses the ball off of the backboard. The basketball should hit the glass at such an angle that it repels to the opposite side of the rim.
2. The player ferociously pursues the basketball and rebounds it at the apex of the jump.
3. The player must catch the basketball before it hits the ground and also land with both feet outside of the lane for the repetition to count.
4. The player then stands on the left side of the basket and repeats the drill.
5. The player repeats the drill 10 times on each side.

Coaching Point

The best rebounders don't just run to the basketball, but they sprint through it. I tell my players to "sprint to it and through it!"

DEFENSIVE REBOUNDING READS

I have seen some deficiencies with the hit-go and boxout techniques. In response to this, I teach a combination of these techniques at my workouts and clinics. This combination requires some basic pivoting reads. Next I will show you three reads for rebounding on the perimeter and two reads for rebounding in the post. Executing the proper reactions to the five defensive rebounding reads will allow you to maintain inside position and keep eye contact with the basketball from the beginning of the shot until the shot hits the rim. Once position and eye contact are maintained, you can more easily pursue the basketball and secure the rebound. This strategy allows you to stay in line with the three keys of defensive rebounding discussed previously. Before you learn the reads and reactions, let's begin with some new terminology for offensive rebounding cuts and basic pivots.

Front-Turn Boxout

From the inside position, execute a front-turn or front-pivot boxout by striking your opponent with a forearm to the chest, pivoting toward the opponent on the foot closest to the direction of their cut, and ending with your posterior against the opponent's thighs and your back to the opponent's chest (see figure 6.1).

Figure 6.1 Front-turn boxout.

Reverse-Turn Boxout

From the inside position, execute the reverse-turn or reverse-pivot boxout by striking your opponent with a bent forearm to the chest, pivoting away from the opponent on the foot closest to the direction of their cut, and ending with your posterior against the opponent's thighs and your back to the opponent's chest (see figure 6.2).

Figure 6.2   Reverse-turn boxout.

Strong-Side Cut

A strong side cut is a perimeter cut in pursuit of a rebound. It is executed by a player in the outside position. It is a cut to the rim but also toward the shooter. For example, if a shot was taken to the right of a player, the player would cut right and then toward the basket (see figure 6.3).

Weak-Side Cut

A weak side cut is a perimeter cut in pursuit of a rebound. It is executed by a player in the outside position. It is a cut toward the rim but away from the shooter. For example, if a shot was taken to the right of a player, the player would cut left and then toward the basket (see figure 6.4).

Figure 6.3 Strong-side cut.

Figure 6.4 Weak-side cut.

Read 1: Perimeter Rebounding

Use the hit-go technique and then read your opponent's reaction. If the opponent does not make a cut for the basketball, quickly turn your attention to pursuing the ball (figure 6.5). Less is more: If you do not have to pivot to secure and maintain inside position, don't waste your time or energy; simply turn your attention to obtaining the rebound.

Figure 6.5 Read 1.

Read 2: Perimeter Rebounding

Use the hit-go technique and then read your opponent's reaction (figure 6.6). If the opponent makes a strong side cut, execute a front-turn boxout.

Figure 6.6 Read 2.

Read 3: Perimeter Rebounding

Use the hit-go technique and then read your opponent's reaction (figure 6.7). If the opponent makes a weak side cut, execute a reverse-turn boxout.

Figure 6.7 Read 3.

PERIMETER READS DRILL

Breakdown

Setup

- Use two players and one basketball.
- Player 1 is on offense and is outside the three-point arc; player 2 is on defense and is inside the lane. The coach has the basketball and is outside the three-point arc.

Execution

1. The coach attempts a shot.
2. When the shot goes up, player 2 sprints to player 1 to box out.
3. Player 1 executes a cut that was established by the coach prior to the drill, but player 2 does not know what type of cut will be used.
4. Player 2 then makes the correct reaction to the cut, executes the proper boxout technique, and pursues the rebound.
   - If player 1 attempts a strong-side cut to the lane in pursuit of the basketball, player 2 executes a front-turn boxout and then rebounds the ball.
   - If player 1 attempts a weak-side cut in pursuit of the basketball, player 2 executes a reverse-turn boxout and then rebounds the ball.
   - If player 1 is stagnant and does not pursue the basketball, player 2 executes the hit-go technique and quickly rebounds the basketball.
5. Players repeat the drill until player 2 makes five consecutive correct perimeter reads and reactions.

Coaching Point

After the correct pivot is executed and inside position is maintained, the player should pursue the basketball by sprinting and securing the ball at the apex of the jump with two hands.

Reads 4 and 5: Post Rebounding

The first three reads dealt with rebounding on the perimeter, but reads 4 and 5 pertain to rebounding on the low block and the lane. As before, use the hit-go technique and read your opponent's reaction (figure 6.8). If the opponent cuts toward the middle of the lane, execute a front-turn boxout. If the opponent cuts toward the baseline, execute a reverse-turn boxout (figure 6.9).

Figure 6.8   Read 4.

Figure 6.9 Read 5.

POST READS DRILL

Breakdown

Setup

- Use two players and one basketball.
- Player 1 is on offense; player 2 is on defense and is inside the lane. The coach has the basketball and is outside the three-point arc.

Execution

1. The coach attempts a shot.
2. When the shot goes up, player 2 sprints to player 1 to box out while player 1 attempts to pursue the basketball.
3. If player 1 attempts a cut to the middle of the lane to pursue the basketball, player 2 executes a front-turn boxout.
4. If player 1 attempts a cut toward the baseline to pursue the basketball, player 2 executes a reverse-turn boxout.
5. If player 2 makes the correct pivot and secures the rebound, that player is awarded 1 point.
6. Players repeat the drill until player 2 has 5 points.

Coaching Point

When a player is boxing out, make sure the hands and arms are above the head in the shape of a field-goal post to prevent the opponent from reaching the basketball.

OFFENSIVE REBOUNDING MANEUVERS

As previously mentioned, offensive rebounds will give your team more possessions. More possessions mean more points, and more points mean more wins! There is nothing more discouraging to a defensive team than working diligently to force a tough, highly contested shot only to have the offense regain possession through a rebound. As an offensive rebounder, your primary goal is to use your peripheral vision to see the basketball and the floor before the shot is taken. This type of vision will give you a head start to the ball because you are moving on the flight of the shot as it leaves the shooter's hands rather than once the shot hits the rim. As the shot goes up, avoid contact and cut in a straight line toward the basketball to secure the rebound by retrieving it at the apex of the jump. Finish by tucking the ball under your chin for security and landing with a wide base for balance. If defensive contact occurs, attempt to break contact and quickly gain separation. It's okay to be boxed out, but it's not okay to remain boxed out. Now let's learn several offensive rebounding maneuvers you can use to prevent being boxed out and to gain separation from the defense.

Fake-and-Go

When cutting to regain inside position for a rebound, use the fake-and-go. The fake-and-go is most applicable when the defense attempts to box out using a reverse-turn pivot. To execute the fake-and-go, look at the basketball and the floor before the shot. Move on the flight of the shot as soon as it leaves the shooter's hands; then sprint directly toward your opponent. From here you have the choice to either fake right followed by a cut to the left to pursue the ball or to fake left followed by a cut to the right to pursue the ball. Once the fake is made, sprint hard to the ball with your hands outstretched and leap high to retrieve the basketball at the apex of the jump. Finish by tucking the ball under your chin for security and landing with a wide base for balance.

FAKE-AND-GO DRILL

Breakdown

Setup

- Use two players and one basketball.
- Player 1 is on offense and is outside the three-point arc; player 2 is on defense and is inside the paint. The coach has the basketball.

Execution

1. The coach attempts a shot.
2. When the shot goes up, player 2 sprints to player 1 to box out while player 1 executes a fake-and-go cut to the basketball for the rebound.
3. Players change positions and repeat the drill until each player has executed 10 repetitions.

Coaching Point

The defender is not actually defending but instead is a tool for instruction. The defender should react to the move as if they've been faked out.

Spin Move

When cutting to regain inside position for a rebound, use the spin move (also called the washing machine). The spin move is most applicable when the defense blocks the offensive player's cut to the rim with contact. To execute the spin move, first look at the basketball and the floor before the shot. Move on the flight of the shot as soon as it leaves the shooter's hands; then sprint directly toward your opponent. When contact occurs, spin 360 degrees in the opposite direction of contact. For example, if the defender strikes you with a forearm to the right shoulder, spin to the left. Once the spin is executed, sprint hard to the ball with your hands outstretched and leap high to retrieve the basketball at the apex of the jump. Finish by tucking the ball under your chin for security and landing with a wide base for balance.

SPIN MOVE DRILL
Breakdown

Setup

- Use two players and one basketball.
- Player 1 is on offense and is outside the three-point arc, player 2 is on defense and is inside the paint. The coach has the basketball.

Execution

1. The coach attempts a shot.
2. When the shot goes up, player 2 sprints to player 1 to box out while player 1 executes a spin move and cuts to the basketball for the rebound.
3. Players change positions and repeat the drill until each player has executed 10 repetitions.

Coaching Point

The defender is not actually defending but instead is a tool for instruction. The defender should react to the move as if they've been faked out.

Straight Cut

When cutting to regain inside position for a rebound, use the straight cut (also known as the go cut). The straight cut is most applicable when the defense attempts to box out using a front-turn pivot or when there is no defender between the offensive player and the basket. To execute the straight cut, first look at the basketball and the floor before the shot. Move on the flight of the shot as soon as it leaves the shooter's hands; then find the open gap and sprint in a straight line toward the basketball with your hands outstretched and leap high to retrieve the basketball at the apex of the jump. Finish by tucking the ball under your chin for security and landing with a wide base for balance.

STRAIGHT CUT DRILL

Breakdown

Setup

- Use two players and one basketball.
- Player 1 is on offense and is outside the three-point arc; player 2 is on defense and is inside the paint. The coach has the basketball.

Execution

1. The coach attempts a shot.
2. When the shot goes up, player 2 sprints to player 1 to box out while player 1 executes a straight cut to the basketball for the rebound.
3. Players change positions and repeat the drill until each player has executed 10 repetitions.

Coaching Point

The defender is not actually defending but instead is a tool for instruction. The defender should react to the move as if they've been faked out.

REFINEMENT DRILLS

You have now learned the proper fundamentals of rebounding. It's time to advance to next section of refinement drills, where you will put your skills to the test in one-on-one drills. This is where the real training begins!

WARTIME DRILL

Refinement

Setup

- Use three players and one basketball.
- The players are inside the lane. The coach is outside the three-point arc with the basketball.

Execution

1. The coach attempts a shot.
2. All three players compete to secure the rebound and score.
3. This is a one-on-one-on-one game and players are competing for themselves.
4. Play does not stop when a basket is made; each player can battle for the basketball and quickly score again. Each basket is awarded one point.
5. There are no fouls; players can grab, push, and contest within reason and without intent of injury.
6. The drill ends when one player has 4 points.

Coaching Point

This is an extremely competitive and physical drill that requires toughness and courage. Be sure to monitor the drill to keep everything under control.

REBOUNDING OVERLOAD DRILL

Setup

- Use 12 players and one basketball.
- Five defensive players are inside the lane and seven offensive players are outside the three-point arc. Offensive players 6 and 7 start at the foul lines extended out of bounds on each sideline of the court.

Execution

1. The coach passes the ball to the offense; the defense reacts by closing out to defend each offensive player man to man (figure 6.10).

2. The offense immediately takes the shot.

3. When the shot is taken, the defense attempts to maintain inside position by boxing out while all seven offensive players pursue the rebound.

4. If the defense secures the rebound, they receive 1 point for their team.

5. Players repeat the drill until the defensive team scores 5 points.

Figure 6.10 Rebounding overload drill.

Coaching Point

This is an overload drill that puts the five defensive players in an extreme disadvantage as they fight to secure the rebound against seven offensive players. Master rebounding in a five-on-five setting before attempting this challenging drill.

REBOUND POUND DRILL

Refinement

Setup

- Use six players and one basketball.
- Three offensive players are on the baseline facing up the court and three defensive players are on the opposite side of the court across the free-throw line with their backs to the offense.

Execution

1. The coach blows the whistle.

2. The three offensive players sprint up the court toward the three defensive players.

3. When the offensive players reach half-court, the coach will blow a second whistle and attempt a shot.

4. When the defense hears the second whistle, they are allowed to turn around and face the charging offensive players (figure 6.11).

5. The defense works to maintain inside position and secure the rebound while the offense pursues the basketball.

6. The team that secures the rebound receives 1 point; then the drill resets as the offense goes to defense.

7. Players repeat the drill until one team earns 7 points.

Coaching Point

Communication is key. Players should be proactive and communicate to their teammates which player they are going to box out.

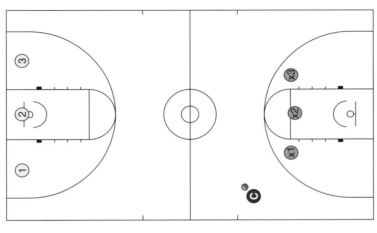

Figure 6.11   Rebound pound drill.

PROTECT THE THRONE DRILL

Setup

- Use six players and one basketball.
- Three defensive players are outside the lane and three offensive players are outside the three-point arc. The basketball is inside the center of the lane.

Execution

1. The coach blows the whistle.

2. The three offensive players fight to pursue the basketball while the three defensive players work to maintain inside position and protect the ball (figure 6.12).

3. If the defense can hold their ground for five seconds, they are awarded 1 point.

4. If the offense can break through and gain possession of the basketball, they are awarded 1 point.

5. Players change possessions each time and continue the game until one team has scored 5 points.

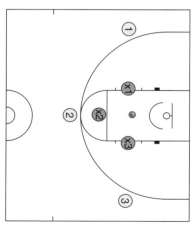

Figure 6.12   Protect the throne drill.

Coaching Point

This a great offensive and defensive rebounding drill. Offensive rebounding point: The offensive team should strive to avoid contact and execute offensive rebounding maneuvers to gain separation from their defenders. Defensive rebounding point: The defensive team should hit the offense early and not wait for the offense to come to them.

NO MISSES FIVE-ON-FIVE DRILL

Refinement

Setup

- Use 10 players and one basketball.
- Five players are on offense and five players are on defense.

Execution

1. Players compete in a five-on-five, full-court game with normal rules, scoring, and guidelines, with one exception.

2. When a team scores, possession does not automatically go to the defensive team. Instead, the basketball is available to whichever team is the first to rebound it.

3. If the offense is first, they may quickly look to score again; if the defense secures the ball, they will change ends of the court for their possession.

4. The team with the most points after 10 minutes wins the game.

Coaching Point

This a great drill that helps players develop the mind-set that every shot could be a missed shot and they should be in the habit of pursuing every rebound.

EVERYONE FOR THEMSELVES DRILL

Refinement

Setup

- Use five players and one basketball.
- The players are inside the lane. The coach is outside the three-point arc with the basketball.

Execution

1. The coach attempts a shot.
2. All five players compete against each other to secure the rebound.
3. When a player obtains the rebound, that player receives 1 point and the drill resets with the coach attempting another shot.
4. The drill ends when one player has 5 points.

Coaching Point

It's okay to be boxed out, but it is not okay to remain boxed out. Extra effort and resiliency are crucial for success in this drill.

BOXOUT BATTLE DRILL

Refinement

Setup

- Use two players.
- The players are back to back in the center circle at half-court.

Execution

1. When the coach says go, the players attempt to push each other outside the half-court circle by using their legs to push back against the opponent (figure 6.13a).

2. The drill ends when one player has been pushed out of the circle (figure 6.13b).

Coaching Point

The lower player has an advantage in this competition. Make sure that the players are in a low stance with a wide base to ensure balance and body control.

Figure 6.13 Boxout battle drill.

Former NBA player Dennis Rodman had a career average of 7 points per game. If you're not familiar with Dennis, you might assume he was a very mediocre player. Despite not being a good scorer, Dennis won five NBA Championships and was inducted into the Naismith Memorial Basketball Hall of Fame. How did this happen? Well, Dennis was arguably the best rebounder of all time. He was always first to the basketball because he made a habit of pursuing every shot as if it would miss. He loved contact and collisions, and he would willingly battle through bigger and stronger opponents. He put his body on the line time and time again by diving on the floor or out of bounds in pursuit of the ball. Dennis embodied all the great attributes of a dominant rebounder, and he took great pride in his role. For a team to be successful, all five players must take the same approach that Dennis did. They must each feel that it's their responsibility to rebound. How can coaches develop this in players? They must emphasize it daily in practice until it becomes natural. Players will ultimately become what coaches emphasize most. Coaches can apply the fundamentals and drills in this chapter to give their teams a great start.

Chapter 7

Individual Defense

I look back at my high school playing days with great fondness. I played for a great coach named Brian Cantrell who is a big mentor in my life. The thing you need to know about Coach Cantrell is that he loved defense. In fact, we would spend the majority of each practice working on individual and team defensive drills. Because of this, we became a very sound defensive team that was well conditioned. To this day, he is the best defensive coach I've been associated with, and I couldn't possibly write this chapter without mentioning him. I remember being at practice once and Coach taking the time to share a thought with me. "Ryan, from time to time I see players in their driveways shooting or working on their ball handling, but you know what? In all my years, I have never driven by someone's home and seen them working on their defense." Coach then chuckled to himself and walked away. As a 15-year-old who wanted to do anything to please my coach, I remember immediately taking this as a challenge. I wanted to be the first player he saw working on their defense, no matter how eccentric I might look to everyone else. Besides being a tremendous tactical and technical coach, Coach Cantrell always knew exactly what to say to get me and my team-mates to buy into the defensive side of the court. To be a great defensive coach, you have to sell it daily to your players just as Coach Cantrell did. It is our job as coaches to teach, cultivate, and develop a love for defense in our players. Be motivational, be creative, and, most importantly, be enthusiastic! I learned all of these things from my coach's great example.

Defense requires astute conditioning, sound fundamentals, and a lot of effort. In this chapter, I explore the fundamentals of man-to-man defense and how to defend an opponent on the perimeter and in the post.

EFFORT

Let's begin with effort. You can't become a great defender without having a high-performance motor inside you, and your effort is that motor. As a coach, I tell my players to work as if they have Ferrari or Lamborghini engines! I see all types of players in my travels; many of them are tall, athletic, and skilled and look like they are built for speed, endurance, and performance, but looks can be deceiving. If I were to "pop the hoods" on some of these high-performance players, there might be lawnmower or golf cart motors inside. Simply put, you can be the most athletic player, but if you don't have a big motor and consistently play with maximum effort and aggressiveness, then you cannot be an elite defender. Effort is the genesis of greatness on the defensive side of the floor. In addition to putting forth effort, it is important to train your body to become a weapon against your opponent. I like to remind my players that the best players are in the best shape. To play at the level of intensity that being a great defender requires, you must prepare your body by being in top condition. You must be able to work harder and longer than your opponent. You might not have control over how tall you are or how fast you can run, but you can always be in the best shape possible each time you step on to the court.

INDIVIDUAL DEFENSIVE DRILLS

The first rule of on-ball defense, whether in the post or on the perimeter, is to always stay between your opponent and the basket. This will help prevent an easy shot, drive, or penetrating pass, and, as we learned in chapter 6, it will help you maintain dominant position for the rebound.

Closeout

When you are defending on the perimeter and your opponent receives a pass, implement what is commonly referred to as a *closeout*. While the pass is in flight, sprint toward your opponent and then break down at the last moment by chopping your feet quickly to decelerate and gather control (see figure 7.1*a*). At the same time, assume an athletic stance with a hand high to be ready to contest a potential shot (see figure 7.1*b*). When closing out, remember to sprint: sprint the first two-thirds of the space between you and your opponent, and then chop your feet the last one-third of the way. This will allow you to arrive at the opponent on balance and ready to defend without momentum leading you in any particular direction.

Figure 7.1 Line closeout.

LINE CLOSEOUT DRILL

Breakdown

Setup

- Use one player.
- The player starts the drill under the rim on the baseline.

Execution

1. The player sprints and closes out at the free-throw line by leading with the right foot and right hand.

2. The player then quickly turns and sprints back to close out at the baseline by leading with the left foot and left hand.

3. The player repeats this for 30 seconds and then completes two more repetitions.

Coaching Point

Remember to tell the player to sprint and then chop! The player should sprint the first two-thirds of the space between the player and the opponent, and then chop their feet the last one-third of space to close out before coming to a complete stop.

Stance

Once your opponent has the basketball on the perimeter, maintain a low and athletic stance with your weight slightly forward on the balls of your feet (figure 7.2). Place your nose in line with your opponent's sternum and fix your eyes on their midsection. This will help you keep your opponent in front of you. The ball handler might fake with their eyes, their feet, or the basketball, but they cannot fake with the body. Wherever the core goes, the opponent must follow. A small cushion of space will also help you keep your opponent in front of you. Always attempt to keep one arm's length of space between you and the ball handler when they are in the triple-threat position or when they are dribbling. If the ball handler picks up their dribble, which is called a *dead ball*, quickly close that gap and pressure the ball handler because they now must remain stationary.

Be Active

A great coach once said that "a defensive player that stays in motion is always ready for motion." Remember to be active with your feet and hands. Chop your feet quickly to remain ready to react to your opponent's movement, and use your hands to mirror the basketball wherever the ball goes. For example, if your

Figure 7.2   Single player defensive stance.

opponent moves the basketball high, your hands mirror the ball high; if the basketball moves low, your hands mirror the ball low. Mirroring the basketball helps you create more deflections and steals, and it can also create a sense of urgency and push the offensive player outside of their comfort zone (see figure 7.3a and b).

Figure 7.3   Mirroring.

ACTIVE DEFENDER DRILL

Breakdown

Setup

- Use one player.
- The player is in a low and athletic stance.

Execution

1. The coach blows a whistle.
2. The player remains in one place and has active feet and active hands for 30 seconds.
3. The player chops the feet quickly and alternates arm movements from the hip to the head.
4. The player completes the drill for 30 seconds and then completes two more sets.

Coaching Point

The player should maintain a low and athletic stance for the duration of the drill. There is a tendency for players to slowly come out of the stance as they become fatigued.

SHADOW DRILL

Breakdown

Setup

- Use two players and one basketball.
- Player 1 begins with a basketball in the triple-threat stance; player 2 closely defends.

Execution

1. Player 1 quickly and randomly moves the basketball from high to low and low to high while gripping the basketball with two hands.
2. While in a defensive stance, player 2 attempts to mirror the basketball with the lead defensive hand and follow it wherever it goes.
3. Players repeat the drill for 30 seconds and then complete two more sets.

Coaching Point

The defensive player mirrors the basketball only with the lead hand (not the back hand). If the offensive player pivots and changes their stance, the defensive player should quickly drop pivot to maintain inside position and also switch the lead hand.

Footwork and Changing Direction

A player's ability to use his or her feet and change directions quickly and assertively is of upmost importance to becoming a good defender. There is nothing an offensive player with the basketball dreads more than competing against an aggressive defender with great footwork. A great on-ball defender has the ability to keep their body between their opponent and the basket, even when the offensive player is on the move and changing directions. Players that have mastered this skill are commonly referred to as *lock-down defenders*. When your opponent uses the dribble and goes on the move, use a step-slide technique to keep your body between the opponent and the basket. To perform the step-slide, start in a low and wide stance with your feet shoulder-width apart, step with the foot that is in the direction you want to go, and slide the opposite foot. For example, if you want to move to the right, step with the right foot first, push off and slide the left foot, and repeat. Keep in mind that your slide foot can never cross the midline of your body (see figure 7.4).

Figure 7.4   Step-slide technique.

Any time your feet are close, your stance narrows and you could lose your balance. To ensure a wide and on-balance stance, take short, choppy steps when using the step-slide technique. Short, choppy steps will get the ball handler off balance, but long extended steps will get you off balance. If your opponent changes direction with the dribble, use the drop-pivot technique to quickly change direction and maintain inside position between your opponent and the basket. For example, if you want to change direction to the right, drop the right foot back and pivot on the left foot; if you want to change direction to the left, drop the left foot back and pivot on the right foot (see figure 7.5).

Figure 7.5 Drop pivot.

LANE SLIDING DRILL

Breakdown

Setup

- Use one player.
- The player faces the basket inside the lane with the outside foot on the lane line.

Execution

1. In a low and athletic stance, the player slides from one side of the lane to the other.

2. The player repeats this for 30 seconds and then completes two more sets.

Coaching Point

The feet should never cross. As the player step-slides across the lane, make sure the slide step never crosses the midline of the body.

CHANGE OF DIRECTION DRILL

Setup

- Use one player.
- The player is in the corner of the court where the baseline meets the sideline.

Execution

1. The player faces the baseline and step-slides laterally to the elbow.

2. On reaching the elbow, the player drop pivots, changes direction, and step-slides to the corner of half-court.

3. On reaching half-court, the player drop pivots, changes direction, and step-slides to the opposite elbow.

4. On reaching the elbow, the player finishes the drill by drop pivoting, changing direction, and step-sliding to the opposite corner of the baseline (figure 7.6).

5. The player repeats the drill three times.

Coaching Point

When they are executing the drop pivot, remind players to pivot from a low stance to a lower one for balance.

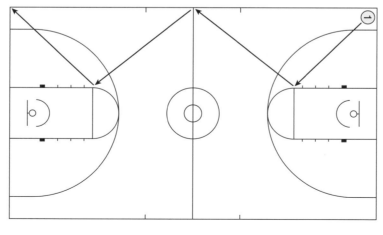

Figure 7.6   Change of direction drill.

DEFENSIVE ORCHESTRA DRILL

Breakdown

Setup

- Use up to six players and one basketball.
- The players stand 10 to 15 feet in front of the coach. If more than one player is participating in the drill, there should be at least an arm's length of space between each player (figure 7.7).

Execution

The coach "leads the orchestra" and issues the following visual commands that the players must quickly follow:

1. Coach points to the ground. The players dive on the ground for the loose ball and shout "my ball!"

2. Coach points right. The players quickly step-slide to the right.

3. Coach points left. The players quickly step-slide to the left.

4. Coach points toward the player. The players quickly drop pivot and step-slide away from the coach.

5. Coach shoots. The players shout "shot" and quickly contest the shot and box out.

Coaching Point

This is a great drill to use daily in practice because it quickly touches on many of the on-ball defensive principles and techniques.

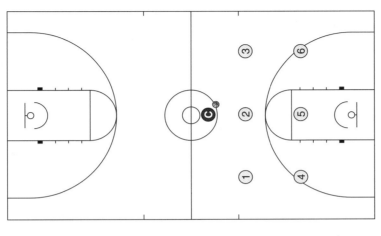

Figure 7.7   Defensive orchestra drill.

Defending the Ball in the Interior

Defending an opponent who has the ball in the interior of the court can be a challenging task. It should be the goal of any defender to not allow the ball to enter the interior by pass, drive, or offensive rebound. But, if you find yourself defending an opponent with the ball in the interior, remember the following tactics:

1. Maintain inside position and force the offensive player to take a contested shot over you. Align your nose to the vertebrae of the ball handler, and keep your hands extended above your head to create a barrier that the offense has to shoot over (see figure 7.8). This wall will lower a shooter's percentages and oftentimes force your opponent to pass.

2. Stay low and wide in your stance to ensure balance, and use your hips to subtly influence and steer the offensive player away from the basket.

3. Be active and keep your feet chopping so you can quickly react to the opponent's moves.

4. If a shot is taken, quickly front pivot and box out with the hands high and secure the rebound at the top of your jump with two hands.

Figure 7.8   Interior on-ball defense.

Deny the Pass

When defending a player without the basketball who is close to the ball handler, enter a deny stance. The purpose of the deny stance is to prevent a pass from being completed to your opponent while also maintaining inside position between your opponent and the basket. When you enter the deny stance, you should always be able to see your opponent and the basketball. Position your body so your chest points to your opponent and your back points to the basketball. While you are in this stance, turn your head so you can see both your opponent and the ball in your peripheral vision. Extend your outside arm into the passing lane with the palm of your hand turned toward the ball handler (see figure 7.9). This will help deter a pass from being thrown or facilitate a deflection or a steal if a pass is thrown.

When implementing the deny stance while guarding an opponent who is posting up in the interior, use all of these teaching points and remember to position the body to take away the middle of the floor. For example, if your opponent is posting up on the low block, fight for the deny position above the low block to force your opponent toward the baseline, where their passing and scoring options are more limited. To discourage a post entry pass, execute what I call the "windshield wiper": move the deny hand vigorously up and down in front of your opponent to take away the passing angle or window (see figure 7.10).

Figure 7.9 Deny the pass on the perimeter.

Figure 7.10 Deny the pass on the post.

DENY THE PERIMETER DRILL

Breakdown

Setup

- Use two players and one basketball.
- Player 1 starts on offense on the low block; player 2 is on defense and positioned between player 1 and the coach. The coach is at the top of the key outside the three-point arc with the basketball.

Execution

1. Player 1 attempts to get open on the wing but must remain on the same side of the court and not cross the middle of the rim.
2. Player 2 attempts to defend player 1 by denying the pass.
3. If the coach completes a pass to player 1, player 1 quickly passes the ball back to the coach and the drill continues; if player 2 gets a steal, player 2 quickly passes the ball back to the coach and the drill continues.
4. Players perform the drill for 30 seconds and then complete two more sets.

Coaching Point

The defensive player should use peripheral vision to maintain eye contact with both the basketball and the offensive player.

DENY THE POST DRILL

Breakdown

Setup

- Use four players and one basketball.
- There is one player on each wing outside the three-point arc and two players are on the low block. There is one player on offense and the other is on defense.
- The offensive player starts the drill on the low block facing the wing; the defensive player begins in a three-quarters deny stance with a hand in the passing lane.

Execution

1. The offensive player works to get open while the defensive player attempts to deny the pass; this continues for 30 seconds (figure 7.11).

2. If the offensive player is not open, the passer on the wing swings the ball to the opposite wing. The offensive player then follows the basketball from one block to the other.

3. If a pass is completed to the offensive player on the block, the defensive player quickly changes to inside position between their opponent and the basket. Once inside position is gained, the offensive player passes the basketball back to the wing and the drill continues.

4. If the defensive player creates a deflection or steals the pass, the defensive player immediately passes the basketball back to the wing and the drill continues.

5. Players repeat the drill for 30 seconds and then complete two more sets.

Figure 7.11   Deny the post drill.

Coaching Point

While in the three-quarters deny stance, the defensive player uses the outside hand to create a barrier by moving the arm up and down like a windshield wiper.

REFINEMENT DRILLS

You have now learned the proper fundamentals of individual defense. It's time to advance to next section of refinement drills, where you will put your skills to the test in one-on-one drills. This is where the real training begins!

ONE-ON-ONE PERIMETER DRILL

Refinement

Setup

- Use two players and one basketball.
- The players begin at the top of the key. Player 1 is on offense with the basketball; player 2 is on defense.

Execution

1. The coach blows the whistle.
2. Player 1 attempts to score while player 2 defends.
3. If player 2 stops player 1 by either creating a turnover or gaining a defensive rebound, player 2 gets 1 point and remains on defense.
4. If player 1 scores, that player switches to defense but does not receive a point.
5. The only way to score a point in this game is to get a stop on defense.
6. The first player to score 10 points wins the game.

Coaching Point

This is a great drill to create excitement and passion on the defensive end because players can score only by getting defensive stops.

DENY THE PASS ON THE PERIMETER DRILL

Refinement

Setup

- Use two players and one basketball.
- Player 1 is on offense on the low block; player 2 is on defense and is positioned between player 1 and the coach. The coach is at the top of the key outside the three-point arc with the basketball.

Execution

1. Player 1 attempts to get open on the wing but must remain on the same side of the court and not cross the middle of the rim.

2. Player 2 attempts to defend player 1 by denying the pass (see figure 7.12).

3. Each possession is 30 seconds and the player attempts to accumulate points.

4. After 30 seconds, the players switch positions.

5. The drill continues until one player scores 20 points.

Figure 7.12 Deny the pass on the perimeter drill.

Defensive Scoring

Deflections: One point is awarded each time a defender creates a deflection. When a deflection is made, the basketball is quickly returned to the coach and the drill continues.

Steal: Two points are awarded each time the defensive player intercepts a pass. When the defender intercepts a pass, the basketball is quickly returned to the coach and the drill continues.

Offensive Scoring

Completed pass: One point is awarded to the offensive player for each successfully completed pass from the coach. On completion of a pass, the player quickly returns the ball to the coach and the drill continues.

Coaching Point

The defensive player should attempt to split the offensive player's feet with their stance so as to remain between the opponent and the basket. Failure to maintain this inside position can lead to a basket cut and easy scoring opportunity.

DENY THE PASS IN THE POST DRILL

Refinement

Setup

- Use four players and one basketball.
- Players 2 and 3 are passers (one on each wing outside the three-point arc); player 1 is on offense and player 4 is on defense (both are on the low block).

Execution

1. Player 1 works to get open on the low block while the defender attempts to deny the pass.

2. If player 1 is not open on that side, the passer swings it to the opposite wing.

3. Player 1 then follows the basketball from one block to the other (figure 7.13).

4. After 30 seconds, player 1 switches to defense and player 4 switches to offense.

5. Players continue the drill until one player has scored 20 points.

Figure 7.13   Deny the pass in the post drill.

Defensive Scoring

Deflections: One point is awarded each time a defender creates a deflection. When a deflection is made, the basketball is quickly returned to the wing and the drill continues.

Steal: Two points are awarded each time the defensive player intercepts a pass. When the defender intercepts a pass, the basketball is quickly returned to the wing and the drill continues.

Offensive Scoring

Completed pass: One point is awarded to the offensive player for each successfully completed pass from the wing.

On completion of a pass, the player quickly returns the ball to the wing and the drill continues.

Coaching Point

Effort and conditioning are crucial in this drill, just as they are crucial to being a good defender. The player that wants it more and is in better shape usually comes out on top. As you coach technique, remember to always emphasize effort as well.

LATERAL TENNIS BALL DRILL

Refinement

Setup

- Use two players and one tennis ball.
- Players stand about 6 feet (1.8 m) apart and face each other; player 2 has the tennis ball. Players are in a low and athletic stance with active feet.

Execution

1. Player 2 tosses the tennis ball to the left or right of player 1.
2. Player 1 quickly slides to the tennis ball and retrieves it on the first bounce.
3. If player 1 retrieves the ball on the first bounce, that player receives 1 point.
4. Player 1 then repeats the drill by tossing the tennis ball to the left or right of player 2.
5. Player 2 quickly slides to retrieve the tennis ball on the first bounce.
6. If player 2 retrieves the ball on the first bounce, that player receives 1 point.
7. Players continue the drill until one player reaches 10 points.

Coaching Point

Players should take short, choppy steps (not long, extended steps) when sliding to the tennis ball. This will ensure balance and body control.

TENNIS BALL LANE SLIDES DRILL

Refinement

Setup

- Use one player and one tennis ball.
- The player is on one side of the lane with the tennis ball in the outside hand at shoulder level.

Execution

1. The player drops the tennis ball from shoulder height outside the lane.
2. The player slides to the opposite side of the lane and back to retrieve the tennis ball before it stops bouncing.
3. If the attempt is successful, the player receives 1 point and then repeats the drill.
4. To beat the drill, the player must successfully complete it seven consecutive times.

Coaching Point

This drill is about active feet and active hands. Players must first focus on having active feet to give them a chance to use their hands. It's feet first and hands second. Much like in the game, our feet put us into positions to use our hands to create deflections and steals.

Scorecard

Junior varsity: 1 to 2 in a row

Varsity: 3 to 4 in a row

All-conference: 5 to 6 in a row

All-American: 7 or more in a row

POST ONE-ON-ONE DRILL

Refinement

Setup

- Use two players, one basketball, and one chair.
- The players are under the basket on the baseline and the chair is in the center of the lane with a basketball placed in the seat.

Execution

1. The coach blows the whistle.
2. Each player on the baseline sprints toward the chair to gain possession of the basketball.
3. The first player to the ball is on offense and the second player is on defense.
4. Once there is a made shot or a defensive stop, the drill restarts.
5. Each made basket is worth 1 point. The first player to score 5 points wins the drill.

Coaching Point

The defensive player should attempt to gain inside position between the opponent and the basket by keeping the hands high and using the hips to nudge the offensive player away from the basket.

In 2005, after winning a national championship with the University of North Carolina Tar Heels, point guard Raymond Felton had his sights set on the NBA draft. He would later be drafted by the Charlotte Bobcats and begin his NBA career. A few weeks before the draft, Raymond chose to visit the NBA Top 100 Camp. This camp is an annual event for the best high school players in the country, and it is loaded with future college and NBA players. Often, current and former NBA players will come to the camp to share their knowledge and mentor these promising young stars. On the first day, Raymond came to the camp dressed in street clothes and observed the talent. At one basket, some of the top guards in the nation were battling in a one-on-one drill. Raymond watched as each player displayed dominant offensive prowess with fancy moves and above-the-rim finishes. These players scored time and time again with ease, but Raymond was not impressed. Actually, he was so annoyed and frustrated by the lack of defense in the drill that he decided to teach these players a lesson. Raymond went onto the court, stopped the drill, and let each player know he was disappointed in the lack of competitive fire or intensity on defense. He then proclaimed that not a single one of them could score on him, and he said he was going to show them the type of defense that wins championships. Each player then took a turn trying to score on him. He stopped each player from scoring, and only a handful of players even got shots off. His demeanor may have been intimidating, but he was able to send a clear message to those players. Learn from Raymond's example and take the same pride and passion for defense to the court when you play!

Chapter 8

On-Court Play

In 2004, the Detroit Pistons won the NBA Championship by defeating a very talented Los Angeles Lakers team. The Lakers were anchored around superstars Shaquille O'Neal and Kobe Bryant, and on paper they seemed to be the more-talented team. How, then, were the Pistons able to win? The Lakers had better players, but the Pistons were the better team. The Pistons played so well as a unit on offense and defense and they executed with such precision that the talent gap didn't matter. Five players who work hard, work smart, and play together can and do beat more-talented teams. The first seven chapters of this book have given you a firm foundation in the fundamentals of basketball. I have covered almost all aspects of the game. You've learned how to shoot, pass, defend, dribble, rebound, move without the basketball, and set and use screens. It's now time to take everything you've learned and transfer it to on-court play. In a game, each team can have five players on the floor at one time. These five players are selected by their skill level and according to their size and position. For easier comprehension, each position in this chapter will have a specific number.

1. Point guard
2. Shooting guard
3. Small forward
4. Power forward
5. Center

Sometimes I see talented players who look great in drills and in recreational basketball but who don't have a good understanding of how to play in an organized basketball game. They know how to shoot, pass, and dribble, but they don't know the proper timing for a set play or the necessary spacing for a fast break, or they don't know how to defend the weak side in a man-to-man defense. To be a productive part of any team, you must have basketball skills *and* an astute knowledge about how to use those skills in a team setting. This chapter provides a basic introduction to set plays and team offense and defense.

SET PLAYS

Set plays are an important part of the offensive arsenals of many teams. Set plays are useful in numerous scenarios. They incorporate choreographed movement through precision cutting and screening between each of the five offensive players. Sets can be used to assist your team in finding an open receiver for an inbound pass or to free up your post player for an open inside shot. They can also be used in late-game moments to give the defense a different look and to put the basketball in your best player's hands. A coach should be prepared with set plays against different defenses and in different game situations. Next, I will review many useful half-court sets against man-to-man and zone defenses as well as various inbound plays on the sideline and the baseline.

SLOB BOX

Inbound Sets Against Man-to-Man Defense

Setup

- Use five players and one basketball.
- Player 1 inbounds the basketball on the sideline. Players 2 and 3 occupy each block and players 4 and 5 are at each elbow.

Execution

1. Player 5 down screens for player 3; player 4 down screens for player 2, who cuts high toward the top of the key. From here, player 1 completes a pass to player 3 (figure 8.1a).

2. Once player 3 receives the basketball, players 2 and 4 space out wide beyond the three-point line on the weak side of the court.

3. Player 5 then immediately sets a back screen for player 1, who cuts toward the rim.

4. Player 3 looks to complete a pass to player 1 for the layup (figure 8.1b).

5. If player 1 is not open, player 3 has the option to hit player 5, who will read the defense and pop or roll to the rim after setting a screen.

Coaching Point

Make sure player 5 sprints to set the back screen for player 1. It is also important that player 1 sets up the screen by first faking high and away and then changing direction and cutting in a straight line toward the rim. These small fundamental details can make a difference in the success of this play.

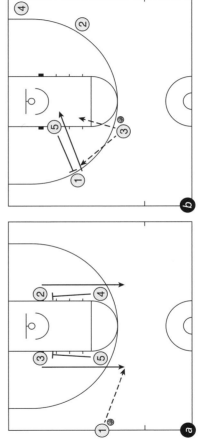

Figure 8.1 Slob box.

BLOB MAN

Inbound Sets Against Man-to-Man Defense

Setup

- Use five players and one basketball.
- Player 4 inbounds the basketball. Players 1 and 2 are outside the top of the key, and player 3 is on the ball-side low block with player 5 directly behind.

Execution

1. When the referee hands player 4 the basketball, players 1 and 2 immediately sprint to each corner while yelling for the ball.

2. At the same time, player 5 sets a screen for player 3.

3. Player 3 then circles back to the middle of the lane, and player 4 lobs the pass over the defense to player 3 for the short-range shot (figure 8.2).

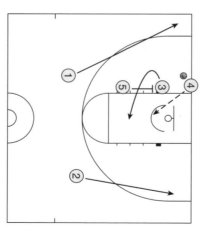

Figure 8.2   Blob man.

Coaching Point

This play is primarily used against a man-to-man defense. Coach the inbound passer to fake a pass to player 1 or player 2 to shift the defense wide and create more space for the lob entry pass to player 3.

BLOB STACK ZONE

Inbound Sets Against Zone Defense

Setup

- Use six players and one basketball.
- Player 3 inbounds the basketball. Players 1, 2, 4, and 5 line up on the ball-side lane in descending order, starting with player 5 at the low block and ending with player 1 at the elbow. One defender is in the middle zone.

Execution

1. When the referee hands player 3 the basketball, player 1 backpedals to outside of the top of the key.

2. Player 2 cuts hard to the ball-side corner.

3. Player 5 screens the middle defender of the zone and player 4 cuts toward the rim.

4. Player 3 then completes a pass to player 4 for the open inside shot (figure 8.3).

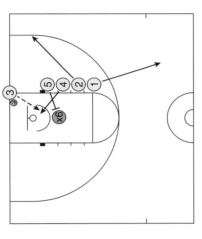

Figure 8.3   Blob stack zone.

Coaching Point

This play is best used against a zone defense. Coach player 5 to post and seek the basketball after setting a screen on the middle defender in the zone. It is often the screener that becomes open in this action.

SLOB ZONE

Inbound Sets Against Zone Defense

Setup

- Use five players and one basketball.
- Player 5 inbounds the basketball on the sideline. Players 1 and 4 occupy each low block and players 2 and 3 are at each elbow.

Execution

1. Player 2 sets a screen on the top part of the 2-3 zone, and player 3 sets a screen on the opposite top side of the zone.

2. Player 1 then flashes high to the key to receive a pass from player 5 for the open outside shot (figure 8.4).

Coaching Point

This play is used against a 2-3 zone. Make sure that the two screeners angle their screens with their backs pointing to the top of the key to create more space and time for the shooter.

Figure 8.4   Slob zone drill.

EAGLE

Half-Court Sets Against Man-to-Man Defense

Setup

- Use five players and one basketball.
- All five players are outside the three-point line. Player 1 is at the top of the key with the basketball, players 2 and 3 are on the wings, and players 4 and 5 are in each corner.

Execution

1. Player 1 initiates the play by dribbling toward player 2. When this happens, player 5 relocates to the opposite corner while player 3 walks their opponent to the low block (figure 8.5a).

2. Once player 5 has relocated to the ball-side corner, player 1 changes direction with the dribble and moves toward the top of the key. As the change of direction happens, player 3 sprints hard toward the wing and calls for the ball (figure 8.5b).

3. As player 3 cuts toward the wing, player 1 executes a pass fake and player 3 plants hard on the outside foot and cuts toward the rim. Player 1 then completes a bounce pass to the cutting player 3 for the layup (figure 8.5c).

Coaching Point

Eagle is a set play that is primarily run against a man-to-man defense. Implement eagle when the defense (or a defender) is overly aggressive and attempting to deny passes.

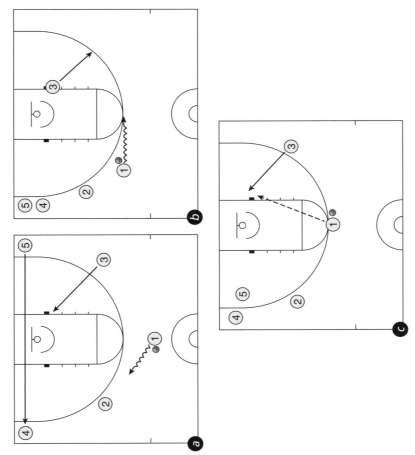

Figure 8.5   Eagle.

PROFESSIONAL SET

Half-Court Sets Against Man-to-Man Defense

Setup

- Use five players and one basketball.

- Player 1 begins at the top of the key with the basketball, player 2 starts under the rim, players 3 and 4 occupy each low block, and player 5 lines up directly behind player 3 (figure 8.6a).

Execution

1. Player 2 can either come off a single screen set by player 3 or a double screen set by players 4 and 5 (figure 8.6b).

- Option 1: Player 2 comes off of the double screen set by players 4 and 5. After setting the screen, player 4 cuts across the lane and comes off a screen set by player 3. Player 1 can then pass to player 2 or player 4 for the shot at the wing (figure 8.6c).

- Option 2: Player 2 comes off of the single screen set by player 3 and cuts to the wing. As soon as player 3 sets the screen, this player cuts across the lane and comes off of the double screen set by players 4 and 5. Player 1 can then pass to player 2 or player 3 for the wing shot (figure 8.6d).

Coaching Point

Sometimes the screeners are the players that will be open. Tell the screeners that if their defender over-helps on the screen, they are no longer screening and they should cut toward the rim and look for the pass to score.

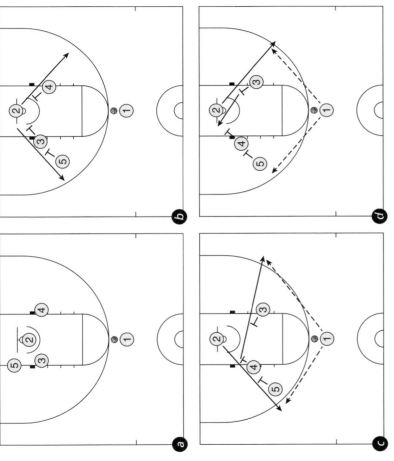

Figure 8.6 Professional set.

LOW-POST DIVE

Half-Court Sets Against Man-to-Man Defense

Setup

- Use five players and one basketball.
- Player 1 is at the top of the key with the basketball, players 2 and 3 occupy the wings, and players 4 and 5 occupy each elbow. The setup is called a one-four high.

Execution

1. Player 3 sets a screen for player 4. Player 4 then cuts to the wing to receive a pass from player 1 (figure 8.7a).

2. As the pass is being completed to player 4, player 3 continues across the lane and sets a screen for player 5, who uses the screen and cuts to the ball-side block.

3. Player 4 executes a post entry pass to player 5 for the high-percentage field-goal opportunity (figure 8.7b).

Coaching Point

Spacing is important in this set play. On the start of the action, make sure all five players are above the foul line and extended to ensure that player 5 is open on the cut.

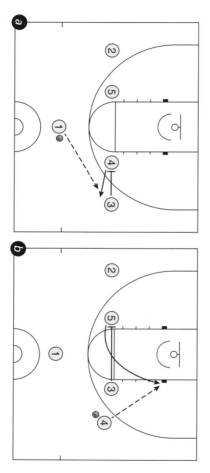

Figure 8.7   Low-post dive.

Half-Court Sets Against Zone Defense

Setup

- Use five players and one basketball.
- Player 1 starts with the basketball at the top of the key, players 2 and 3 occupy each wing, and players 4 and 5 are at each block.

Execution

1. Player 1 passes to player 3. Player 1 then cuts to the ball-side corner. Player 2 fills the unoccupied spot at the top of the key, and player 5 lifts high to the ball-side elbow (figure 8.8a).

2. To complete the play, player 3 makes a pass to player 5 at the elbow. While the pass is in the air, player 4 cuts toward the ball side. Player 5 then delivers a pass to player 4 for the inside shot opportunity (figure 8.8b). If player 4 is not open, player 5 looks for an open teammate or creates a shot to take.

Coaching Point

In a zone, each defender guards a particular area on the court and not a certain player. The purpose of this play is to overload the ball side in an attempt to outnumber the defensive players and create an open scoring opportunity.

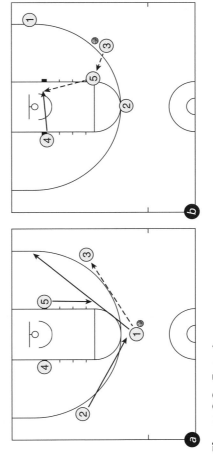

Figure 8.8 Zone 1.

ZONE 2

Half-Court Sets Against Zone Defense

Setup

- Use ten players and one basketball.
- Player 1 dribbles the ball to the wing. Player 2 starts in the corner, players 3 and 4 occupy each block, and player 5 begins on the weak-side wing.

Execution

1. Players 2 and 3 switch spots; then, player 1 passes to player 3 on the ball-side corner (figure 8.9a).

2. While the pass is in the air to player 3, player 4 sets a back screen on player x5 and player 2 sets a back screen on player x2. Player 5 then cuts through the middle of the lane and receives a pass from player 3 for the inside shot (figure 8.9b).

Coaching Point

This play is used against a 1-3-1 zone defense. Timing is very important, and the two back screens must be initiated while the pass from player 1 to player 3 is in the air and not after player 3 receives the pass.

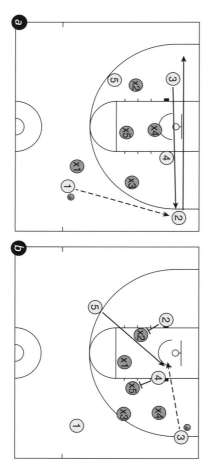

Figure 8.9 Zone 2.

TEAM OFFENSE

The offensive team should be looking for quick and easy scoring opportunities before the opponent has a chance to retreat and set up their defense. These high-percentage early scoring opportunities are called *fast breaks* or *primary breaks*.

Fast Break

Most disciplined teams are taught how to properly run the floor to facilitate these quick and easy points. As shown in figure 8.10, each player has a specific responsibility on the fast break. In addition to these responsibilities, keep in mind that it is the job of every player to sprint the floor, maintain proper spacing, and communicate. The 4 and 5 positions are interchangeable, as are the 2 and 3 positions. The job of the 4 and 5 positions is first to rebound the basketball. If player 4 obtains the rebound, player 5 immediately sprints up the middle of the court and seals their defender at the front of the rim. Player 4 looks to quickly pass the basketball to the position 1 guard. As this is happening, players 2 and 3 run wide near the sideline until they reach the corner of the court where the baseline meets the sideline. The purpose of running wide up the sideline is to create more space between each offensive player, thus making the defense's job much tougher. The position 1 guard tries to make a hit-ahead pass to player 2, 3, or 5 for the open inside or outside shot, or player 1 can dribble up the court if none of these options are open. Player 4 finishes out the break by trailing behind to the weak side of the court. With the fast break, time is of the essence. It is faster to advance the basketball with a pass than with the dribble. If the advantage is there, look to score quickly by passing the basketball up the floor and finding the open player. The more time it takes, the more likely it is that the defense will recover. The fast break lanes in the following diagrams are an important part of the strategy for creating space and open scoring opportunities, and they should be implemented after every defensive rebound and after any quick change of possession.

PRIMARY BREAK DRILL

Breakdown

Setup

- Use five players and one basketball.
- All five players are lined up across the baseline.
- As soon as everyone is in place, the coach takes a shot.
- Player 4 rebounds the basketball and makes a pass to player 1. Player 4 then runs the floor to the opposite three-point arc.
- Player 1 advances the basketball up the court either by pass or dribble.
- Players 2 and 3 run wide and up each sideline to the corner and outside the three-point line.
- Player 5 runs directly to the rim and looks for the basketball and an easy basket.

Execution

1. When the shot goes up, player 4 retrieves the rebound and outlet passes to player 1. At the same time, players 2 and 3 sprint wide up the sidelines and player 5 sprints up the middle of the court and toward the rim (figure 8.10a).

2. During the first trip up the court, player 1 will pass ahead to player 5 for the layup. After each made shot, the drill will reset and each player will line up across the baseline again and wait for the coach to shoot the basketball.

3. The second option is to pass ahead to player 2 for the perimeter shot or drive (figure 8.10b).

4. The third option is to pass ahead to player 3 for the perimeter shot or drive (figure 8.10c).

5. The fourth option is for player 1 to dribble up the court and attack toward the basket for a layup (figure 8.10d).

6. The fifth option is for player 1 to dribble up the court and then pass to player 4, who is trailing the break, for the jump shot (figure 8.10e).

7. Players complete all five options to finish the drill.

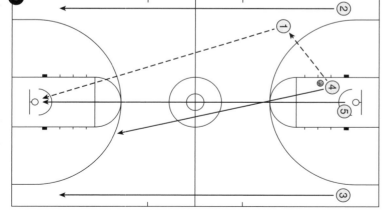

Figure 8.10 Primary break.

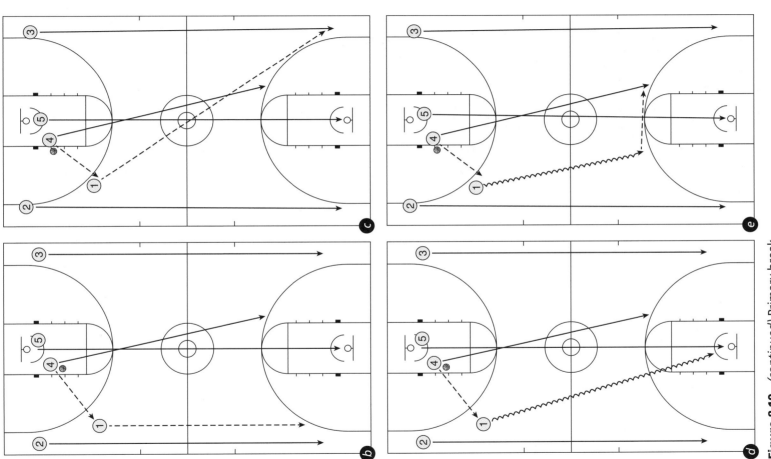

Figure 8.10 *(continued)* Primary break.

Coaching Point

Each player should be sprinting as fast they can. To elevate the drill and to hold each player accountable, I often time the drill. Players must complete all five options within a certain time period.

Motion Offense

The motion offense is one of the most commonly used offenses in basketball, and it can be seen at almost every level of play. The name says it all: the motion offense is all about constant player and ball movement. Players are able to move freely on the court and make their own reads and reactions; they are governed by only a few foundational rules. These rules help the continuity of the offense and help open up the floor for scoring opportunities near the basket. The constant free-flowing motion offense is very difficult to defend, and it is one of the few offenses that is successful against man-to-man and zone defenses alike. There are many variations of the motion offense, but the focus in this chapter is on the open-post motion offense. This type of motion is best suited for a team with smaller, quicker players because it brings all five players outside the three-point arc and stretches the defense. When first introducing youth players to the motion offense, I always begin with the open-post motion offense because it provides a good foundation for more advanced variations. Using the following diagrams, you will learn how to pass, cut, and replace; these are the basics of the motion offense. Once you master these skills, the motion offense can really take flight; many teams apply screening, dribble-drive reads, and other options.

The purpose of the motion offense is to create opportunities to score near the basket.

MOTION OFFENSE

Breakdown

Setup

- Use five players and one basketball.
- Players align themselves outside the three-point arc in positions 1 through 5 as shown in the diagram. Players occupy these positions for the duration of the offense because this positioning maintains 15 to 18 feet (4.6-5.5 m) between each player. This spacing is beneficial for opening up the lane for drives, penetrating passes, and cuts.

Execution

1. In the diagram, player 1 has the option to pass to player 2 or player 3.

2. If player 1 passes to player 3, player 1 must cut to the rim.

3. As player 1 cuts to the rim, player 2 replaces player 1 at the top of the key, player 4 replaces player 2 at the wing, and player 1 replaces player 4 in the corner (figure 8.11).

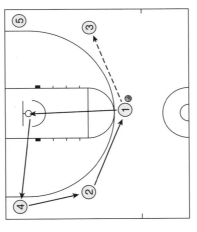

Figure 8.11 Motion offense.

Coaching Point

The cutter always replaces in the opposite direction of the pass. For example, if the cutter passes to the right, they will replace the left corner following the cut.

(continued)

Motion Offense (continued)

MOTION OFFENSE VARIATION 1

In the diagram, player 3 has the option to pass to player 2 or player 5. If player 3 passes to player 5, then player 3 must cut to the rim. As player 3 cuts to the rim, player 2 replaces player 3 on the wing, player 4 replaces player 2 at the top of the key, player 1 replaces player 4 at the wing, and player 3 replaces player 1 in the opposite corner (figure 8.12).

Coaching Point

A simple rhyming phrase to help players remember the rules and the order of operations in the motion offense is "pass, cut, replace, and keep space." When a pass is made, the passer cuts and then everyone looks to replace the open position and keeps 15 to 18 feet (4.6-5.5 m) of space.

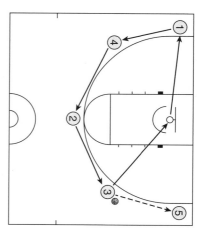

Figure 8.12 Motion offense variaton 1.

MOTION OFFENSE VARIATION 2

Player 5 passes to player 2, immediately cuts to the rim, and continues by replacing the spot that player 5 just occupied. The corner-to-wing pass is the only pass in which the cutter does not replace opposite; instead, the player returns to the spot they first occupied (figure 8.13).

Coaching Point

When cutting to the rim, a player should be disciplined by staying low, keeping their eyes on the basketball at all times, and showing a target with their hands for the passer. To gain a head start on the defender, the player uses the fake and go. To cut to the left, the player first fakes to the right. To cut to the right, the player first fakes to the left.

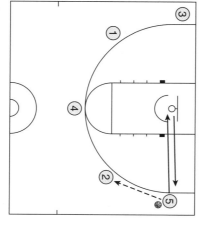

Figure 8.13 Motion offense variation 2.

MOTION OFFENSE VARIATION 3

Player 2 has the option to pass to player 4 or player 5. If player 2 passes to player 4, player 2 must first cut to the rim. As player 2 is cutting to the rim, player 5 replaces player 2 at the wing, player 2 replaces player 5 in the corner, and thus the pattern continues (figure 8.14).

Coaching Point

When replacing a position nearest the basketball, the player uses a cut, such as a V-cut, to get open first. Replacing without incorporating an offensive cutting maneuver allows the defender to deny the pass.

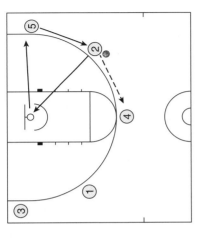

Figure 8.14 Motion offense variation 3.

MOTION OFFENSE VARIATION 4

Player 4 has the option to pass to player 1 or player 5. If player 1 and player 5 are not open, then they should immediately cut to the rim. As 1 and player 5 are cutting to the rim, player 2 replaces player 5 and player 3 replaces player 1. Players 1 and 5 finish out their cuts by replacing the corner positions (figure 8.15).

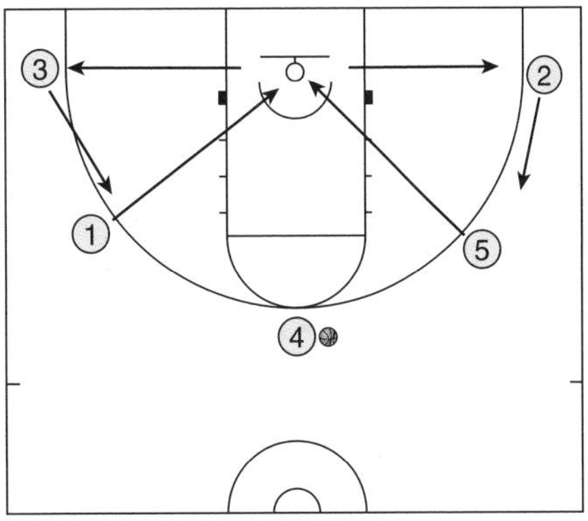

Coaching Point

Constant movement is vital in the motion offense. Any time the player nearest the basketball is not open, that player should immediately cut to the rim so a teammate can replace and facilitate the pass. Players also have the option to screen for one another to continue the motion offense.

Figure 8.15 Motion offense variation 4.

MOTION 15 DRILL

Setup

- Use five players and one basketball.
- Player 1 starts at the top of the key with a basketball, players 2 and 3 are positioned on each wing, and players 4 and 5 begin in each corner.

Execution

1. The five players run their motion offense by passing, cutting, and replacing until they complete 15 passes.

2. After the 15th pass, one player completes a pass to another player who is cutting to the basket for a layup.

3. Players repeat the drill five times.

Coaching Point

There should be 15 to 18 feet (4.6-5.5 m) between each player. To help reinforce this, use tape or cones to mark the court at the top of the key, each wing, and each corner.

TEAM DEFENSE

You learned the fundamentals of individual defense in chapter 7; now you must build an understanding of how to play defense in the team environment. Great team defenses force their opponents to commit more turnovers and shoot at lower percentages from the field, and they limit their opponents to one shot. Great defense doesn't win games; great *team* defense wins games.

There are two categories of team defense: zone and man to man.

Zone Defense

In a zone defense, each defender is responsible for a specified area or zone on the court; the zone can vary depending on where the basketball is on the floor. Zone defenses can be beneficial if your team is smaller or not as athletic or if the opposing team doesn't shoot well from the outside. Some of the more popular zone defenses are the 2-3 zone (figure 8.16), the 3-2 zone (figure 8.17), and the

1-3-1 zone (figure 8.18). The 2-3 zone packs more players inside and helps keep the opposing team outside of the paint. The 3-2 zone helps perimeter players better defend the basketball and stop dribble penetration. The 1-3-1 zone, with its unorthodox setup and trapping, can disrupt and confuse an offensive team.

The zone defense certainly has its advantages, but it is my opinion (and many of my colleagues agree) that it should not be taught until players have a good understanding of team man-to-man principles. All too often, players in youth leagues are playing only zone defense to the detriment of their fundamental defensive skills. They simply are not getting enough repetition to develop footwork, body control, reaction time, and positioning because they are always packed into a zone. The root of this problem is coaches at the youth level who misunderstand their role and think winning is a higher priority than development. The zone defense forces their young, small opponents to shoot from the outside, where their percentages are minimal, giving the team a better chance to win. Unfortunately, this strategy will strain defensive improvement. To improve defensive development, I encourage youth basketball directors to use only man-to-man defense. I want young players to learn how to play defense and guard opponents; I don't want them to only learn how to defend an area. Zone defense has its place in basketball, but not in youth basketball.

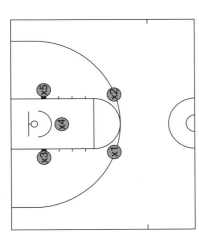

Figure 8.16 2-3 Zone defense.

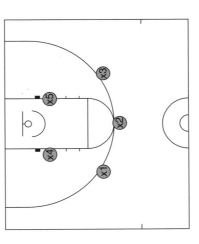

Figure 8.17 3-2 Zone defense.

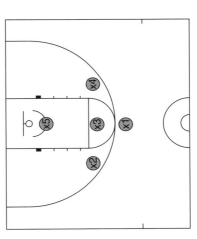

Figure 8.18 1-3-1 Zone defense.

Man-to-Man Defense

In a man-to-man defense, each defender is responsible for a designated player from the opposing team. Being a proficient man-to-man defensive team requires effort, communication skills, great footwork, and knowledge about proper defensive positioning. In addition to defending their opponent, each defender also takes on additional responsibilities depending on where the basketball is on the court. Each player works diligently to individually defend their opponent, but players also provide support to one another as a team. Understanding team man-to-man defensive positioning is crucial to success as teams play together as one cohesive unit. Here I cover the following three positions:

1. On-ball position: A defensive player assumes this position when defending the offensive player with the basketball. This position puts defensive pressure on the ball handler and stops dribble penetration.

2. Deny position: A defensive player assumes this position when the player is one pass away from the basketball. The deny position prevents a pass from the ball handler to their man and provides support to the on-ball position at the risk of a dribble drive.

3. Weak-side position: A defensive player assumes this position when the player is two or more passes away from the basketball. This position provides support on the second level of the team defense. This position discourages penetrating passes and dribble drives while the player is still occupying their opponent.

ON-BALL POSITION

Breakdown

Setup

- Use ten players and one basketball.
- When setting up a man-to man-defense, each player is responsible for defending a player on the opposing team.
- Attempt to match players by similar height and speed.

Execution

1. Player x1 is defending the basketball (figure 8.19).

2. Players x2 and x3 are one pass away and are in deny position.

3. Players x4 and x5 are two passes away and are in weak side position.

Coaching Point

When defending the ball handler, player x1 should be in a low and athletic stance with the arms extended and should maintain inside position. The goal of the on-ball defender is to give constant pressure by mirroring the basketball with their hand(s) and influencing the ball handler to go in the direction of their weak hand.

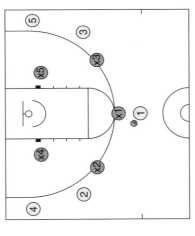

Figure 8.19 On-ball position.

DENY POSITION

Breakdown

Execution

If the ball is on the wing, player x2 guards the basketball while players x1 and x4 are in deny position and players x3 and x4 are in deny position and players x3 and x5 are in weak side position (figure 8.20).

Coaching Point

When in the deny position, a player should take a stance that enables them to see their opponent and the basketball. The player positions the body so the chest points to the opponent and the back points to the basketball. While in this position, the player turns the head so they can see the opponent and the ball with their peripheral vision. In addition, the outside arm is in the passing lane with the palm of the hand turned toward the ball handler to prevent a pass or to more easily intercept a pass if one is thrown. Another responsibility of a player in the deny position is to provide support to the on-ball defender in case of a dribble drive. To help with this, the defender should be two steps off their opponent and toward the ball.

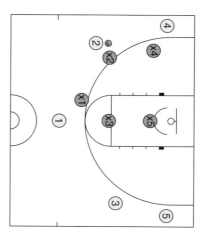

Figure 8.20 Deny position.

WEAK-SIDE POSITION

Breakdown

Execution

If the ball moves to the corner, player x4 guards the basketball while player x2 is in the deny position. Players x1, x3, and x5 are all two or more passes away and are in weak side position (figure 8.21).

Coaching Point

Players in the weak side position should be in a low and athletic stance with their arms extended and they should be two steps below the line of the basketball. These players maintain sight of their opponents and the ball by turning their heads and using their peripheral vision. Players in the weak side position support their teammates in case of a penetrating pass, cut, or drive.

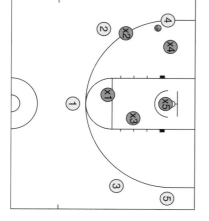

Figure 8.21 Weak-side position.

DRIBBLE DRIVE HELP EXECUTION

Breakdown

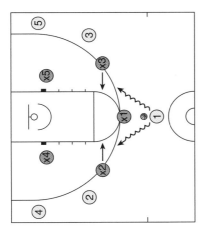

Figure 8.22 Dribble drive help execution.

Execution

If a defender is one pass away from the basketball, this player must provide support against a dribble drive. If an opponent drives in their direction and help is needed, the player step-slides to close off the gap to the basket (figure 8.22).

Coaching Point

It is important that the players in the deny position are two steps away from their opponents so they can more easily react and close the gap to the dribble drive.

DENY THE POST

Breakdown

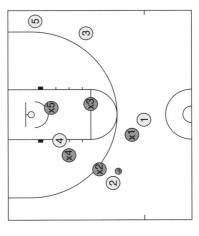

Figure 8.23 Deny the post.

Execution

If the offense uses a post player, the post defender denies the pass by fronting their opponent. In the diagram, player x2 is defending the ball while player x1 is in deny position. Player x4 is fronting and denying the pass while players x5 and x3 are in weak side position. If there is no pass to player 4, player 5 provides help and support (figure 8.23).

Coaching Point

When executing an all-out front on a post player, the defender should position the body between the basketball and the opponent, keep the inside arm bent and in contact with the offensive player, and keep the outside hand high to discourage or deflect a pass. The player's stance should be low and wide to maintain balance and body control.

SHELL DRILL

Breakdown

Setup

- Use 10 players and one basketball.
- Five players are on offense and five players are on defense. The offensive players spread out; player 1 is at the top of the key, players 2 and 3 are at each wing, player 4 is in the corner, and player 5 is on the low block. The five defenders then match up man to man (figure 8.24a).

Execution

This a great drill for learning and reinforcing proper defensive position. The coach is in charge of the drill and tells the offensive team when and where to pass the basketball. After every pass, the coach reviews each defensive player's position and makes any corrections before instructing the offense to make another pass. Players complete passes to all positions a minimum of three times; then, defense and offense switch and repeat the drill.

Coaching Point

To take the drill a step further, add the dribble and instruct players to drive at random times; this allows you to evaluate the defense's ability to react, close gaps, and stop penetration.

1. Drill action 2: basketball on wing defensive positions (figure 8.24b)
2. Drill action 3: basketball in corner defensive positions (figure 8.24c)
3. Drill action 4: basketball on opposite wing defensive positions (figure 8.24d)
4. Drill action 5: basketball in post defensive positions (figure 8.24e)

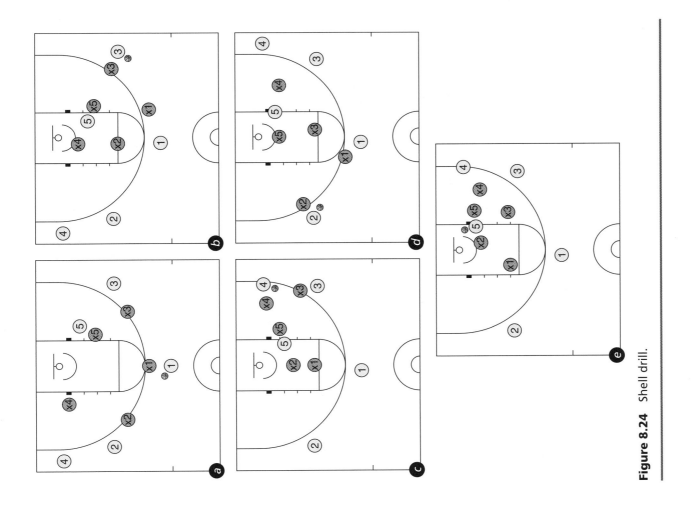

Figure 8.24 Shell drill.

It takes time and repetition to perfect all of the fundamentals you learned in this book. Great teams have players that are not only dedicated to improving their own game but also committed to improving as a team. How much time outside of organized practice do you spend with your teammates working together to get better? Basketball is a team sport, and individual skills and team skills both require sustained effort. Make it a priority to better yourself and better your team.

CONCLUSION

As we come to the end of *Basketball Essentials*, I would like to share one more story with you. At the beginning of many of my camps, I ask players what kinds of dogs they have at home. Of course there are various responses. Then I ask players what kind of dog they think they should be on the court. I usually shout out my answer before they have a chance to respond: "You should be a pit bull! You've got to play like a pit bull and not a Yorkie if you want to thrive in this game. You have to constantly be on the attack!" Basketball is not a girl's game; it's a man's game. Basketball is not a boy's game; it's a woman's game. You have to think and play bigger than you are. This mind-set is absolutely necessary!

This reminds me of a question that a player recently asked me about NBA MVP Stephen Curry: "Ryan, how does Stephen Curry feel about being the smallest player on the court?" I answered with a laugh. "I'm not sure how Steph feels, but I personally don't think he knows that he is the smallest player on the court. He thinks he's the biggest and baddest player each and every time he takes the floor. Stephen Curry plays like a pit bull!" If you want to dominate on the court, you must have a dominant mind-set.

As you take the next steps in improving your game, please remember to set your goals on the process and not on the prize. Do not set a goal of making your high school team or getting a college scholarship. Instead, set your sights on being the hardest worker each and every time you step on the basketball court; then, everything will take care of itself. I've focused on many basketball skills in this book, but the most important skill of all is your work ethic. If your work ethic is your greatest skill, your potential will be unleashed. Basketball essential greatness should be your focus. Don't stop at learning the concepts in this book; seek to refine and master them!

May God bless you on your basketball journey! If I can help you or your team in any way, please contact me by e-mail at ryan@goodsonbasketball.com.

About the Author

Ryan Goodson is a world-renowned coach and clinician of basketball skill development. Since 2009 he has trained more than 15,000 players from the youth to the professional levels and has conducted clinics in 30 states and 5 countries. Goodson is widely sought after to direct youth basketball camps across the globe because of his engaging teaching style and dynamic demonstrations.

Goodson directed the Stephen Curry Skills Academy in 2011 and is consistently contracted to direct camps for the United States Basketball Association. He has also developed a huge basketball following online. His instructional videos have been viewed more than five million times worldwide. Goodson earned a bachelor's degree in health promotion from Appalachian State University.